The Big Secrets

*Ten Things Every Young Person Should
Know About and Why*

By
G. V. Loewen

℀

Strategic Book Publishing and Rights Co.

Strategic Book Publishing and Rights Co.
12620 FM 1960, Suite A4-507
Houston, TX 77065

www.sbpra.com

For information about special discounts for bulk purchases, please contact Strategic Book Publishing and Rights Co. Special Sales, at bookorder@sbpra.net.

ISBN: 978-1-63135-234-8

Design: Dedicated Book Services, (www.netdbs.com)

to our future daughter: may she know everything she needs and wants to know.

Contents

A brief epilogue addressed to adults

Preface:
Why Write a Book Like This?

Kids are less than human. Think about it: you can be assaulted with no legal recourse, emotionally and psychologically abused without any help, denied the basic rights of citizens, and be forced to do things that adults don't have to do. Although you might have fewer responsibilities, being younger than eighteen in most places can be a real drag. Why is it like this?

To be human is to be social. To be fully human is to be fully social. Kids are not fully social. They have not learned all the things they need to function in society. That said, has anyone? If kids are less than human because they do not know quite enough to fully participate in our society, where are the thresholds? How much is enough? And why do adults, who after all run the world, often seem to be doing such a poor job of it? Do we really know what we are doing, or do adults just practice a different form of make-believe than do children? And why are adolescents still treated as little kids under many laws and by many social norms? Why is around the age of eighteen to twenty-one seen to be enough? Enough of what?

This book is about all the stuff we hide from you. It's about the secrets of not only being an adult, or at least pretending to be one, it's also about the lies and abuses we suffer upon you to maintain our control and force you to behave the way we want you to. It's about the way in which the world keeps on rolling as it does. It's about why there sometimes seems to be little effort on our part to make things better, even though we are supposed to know things you don't. All these things together are the *Big Secrets*, and I am going to share them with you.

Why do this? I think when you have finished reading this short book, you will agree that it's better to know than not, no matter how ugly the truth is, or how much you might already suspect but don't want to believe. It will help your life, even if the world around you does not change. You are part of the world, so any change you can make for the better does in fact make a better world. But you need to know a few things before you think about changing. What direction might you take and why? The reason why we lie to you is simply about directions. The reason why we treat you as less than human is because often we are actually as bewildered and frustrated and powerless as you. These are not excuses. I think you'll find that the topics I am going to talk about in this book cannot bear excusing. I am just going to lay it out, and you can come to your own direction. And while I think you're going to find some tools for new directions here, it's still only *sort* of your life—and definitely not your world. Not yet.

But think about when you suddenly are an adult. It might only be a few short years from now. What will that mean? What are you going to do? Does much of what you are taught by parents and teachers and other sources like media prepare you for being an adult? What does adulthood mean? There are a number of ways to answer such a question, but the most important one has always been: knowing how to live by the rules of whatever society or culture you find yourself flung into. Nobody asks to be born, so when we abuse you or lie to you, we conveniently forget that fact. It's one of those ultimate facts of human existence.

We all got here in the same way, and none of us had any say in it. So does growing up mean trading the role of slave for the role of master? Well, not quite. But in the most general sense, being an adult means being not only a rule-follower, but a *rule-supporter*. We don't even have to like the rules, but we have to agree to abide by them and take them as our own. You only have to learn the rules and attempt to live by them. Teens and younger children are always questioning the rules. It is precisely this *lack* of questioning that defines the role of adult. You question authority; we do not.

That sounds really stupid. How could a mature adult simply lie down and do or take whatever is asked of them? This, too, is a question that has many answers. In exploring it in the following pages, we will find out why adults act the way they do, and why most kids are rightfully suspicious of becoming an adult. Not that I want you to give up and stay an adolescent forever. Our modern society already allows persons way older than eighteen to behave like they are ten. That, in fact, is one of the reasons why you might think we are clueless, or hypocrites, or behave no better than kids. But there is a crucial difference between adults behaving like teenagers and actually being one. Adults always return to the adult world after our short flights from it. You can stay as you are, and no one, for the moment, expects more of you.

This absence of expectation is also part of the problems we will explore together. It repeats the key difference between adulthood and childhood. We are expected to support the rules and expected to bend or even break them in times and places where other rules fall into place. You see, an adult can break the rules without questioning their authority. We know we are in the wrong. To *not* know that is to still be a kid.

So there are people who know the rules, people who don't, and then there are also the rules themselves. Where do they come from? Who makes them and why? Why these rules and not others? And what is the purpose of having rules at all? Again, no excuses; we want to know what's what.

In order to figure these questions out without either excusing them or pretending that they are the best we can do, I want to borrow from you some of your questioning skills. This isn't the "Why is the sky blue?" kind of question that a young child, full of wonder and delight, wants and needs to ask. These questions are of the same species as the toughest scientific questions that adults ask and have asked for millions of years. No, I want to ask with you the kind of questions that lead to critique and social change, the ones in league with the toughest *philosophical* questions adults have asked for thousands of years.

To ask *this* kind of question you must put on a real game face. You have to be prepared for resistance of all kinds. And because life and the world are much more than a game—the stakes are way too high to be counted as mere statistics, like in sports—the sources of resistance to your questions have an intense interest in not letting you know much about them. You have to be prepared to push your way in and not take any simple "no" for an answer. You already know what happens to people who question. But I think after reading this book you will be better equipped. You will know more about the kinds of questions you need to be asking, both of yourselves and of adults. And you'll know better how to ask them, so that adults don't feel as threatened and react badly. Most of us need to ask the same questions. It is just that we have lived longer and we might ask them a little differently, or, as is most often the case, we will have lost the ability to ask them at all.

If that is the case, you don't want to end up like us. Of course, it is possible that none of this matters. Human beings will continue to act badly, foment evil, and the species may ultimately be destroyed after much personal and social suffering. No life beyond life. No truth beyond experience. But I think no matter what you might believe in, there is a common credo that makes us human and that makes humans the same. We are all in the same boat. We did not, in any sense, choose to be born, and we do not, in the general sense, choose to die. Yet our deaths make us the same, and our lives make us different. Our mortality unites us; our experiences divide us. It is this paradox that defines the human condition. What it means to be human is to be forced to think this through with each other, and that means asking a lot of questions and not taking anything for granted. If adults have apparently lost the ability to do that, it is *we* who are less than human, and not you.

One final thing before we begin. It is never easy for a philosopher like me to communicate well. It may be that thinkers spend way too much time thinking about things and way too little time thinking with other people. Whatever the case, I promise to try to speak to you in as plain a language as possible, while at the same time to not be condescending. That is, I will try to get complex points across in a way that is simple but without dumbing down. As well, I will try to never make you feel stupid. But you can help me out. Reading a book is actually a two-way street, and the reader is as active as the book. Though I will attempt to define any words that might be unfamiliar to you, if you find that I did not quite get it, or you didn't, then it won't hurt to look up the word or idea in question. Online dictionaries make this simple. I'm going to stay away from references–this is not a scientific text—and name-dropping. I don't have anything I need to prove to you about who I am or what I've done. What I want to do is encourage you to never give up your fullest humanity in the face of authority or in the absence of courage.

1. The Secrets of Sex (and love)

‹‹

Let's talk about sex. Sex is good. Sometimes it is more than good, but that is not the real point. Starting out with this topic is an obvious choice. Most teens are, to say the least, intrigued by sex, some even obsessed by it. Adults, by the way, are no different, even if we pretend to be. But adults are jealous about sex. We want to keep it to ourselves. Is this because it is so good we can't bear to share it? Or is there another, more shadowy reason?

Actually there are two major categories of reasons why adults mostly shudder when they hear about adolescents exploring their own sexuality. One set of reasons makes sense and is rational, insofar as it goes. The other set is selfish, resentful, and irrational. Let's take a look at the better set first.

Unwanted pregnancies, sexually transmitted diseases, addiction, and assault are the usual suspects that are mentioned as reasons against sex. Note that these are all secondary effects of sex, and do not necessarily follow from having sex. In fact, one can enjoy healthy and safe sex without any of these coming up. You cannot say the same thing for drugs, and this is the main reason why there is a clear difference between sex and drugs, but more on that later. Adults are concerned about teen sexuality because we imagine that teens don't know enough about it to prevent the hazards from appearing. Not your fault if you don't of course, because where does the presence or absence of needed information come from? If we as adults are not forthcoming about sex info, you are not going to find it. Listening to older peers might help a little, but where did they get their information from?

With the advent of the Internet, things are a lot easier than when I was your age, and a lot better. I mean the information sites, not necessarily the erotic sites, though you can get an education of sorts from them as well!

It is also the case that adults can suffer all of the same negative consequences of sexual activity as adolescents. We protect ourselves more from them than you do, but only because we have the combination of more experience and—and this is what really counts—we have full access to sexual information by law and by our social role. That is, we do not deny ourselves under the laws we make. Try going into a sex store if you are under eighteen, or even under twenty-one in some areas. Service and sales are treated like selling alcohol to a minor, though I bet sex stores are not under the kind of surveillance that liquor stores are. If you look young, you might have to show ID even if you are far older than these standard age thresholds, just like at a liquor store.

So much for the law. Even more important is that when you are 'of age,' you are seen as self-responsible. So if you want to go out and get an STD (sexually transmitted disease), you can. It's none of my business. Though we have to pay health care costs for people who we call irresponsible, young and old, we accede to the somewhat strange idea that adults can get themselves into as much trouble as they want—often times at others' expense—because that is their right. It is part of our definition of freedom. Adults are free to act as they choose because they are supposedly aware of the consequences. This logic follows even to the point of real crimes, like rape and murder, where the law can only react with consequences, or sanctions, and much more rarely does it prevent crime. Indeed, we might think that the law and its officers and citizens do not even know when they have prevented a crime, simply because it never happened.

We actually rely not so much on the law for civil society but on our social role behaviors. We assume adults will act like responsible adults—plenty of exceptions here, no doubt—and we go about our own business in the same manner. Remember, to be an adult you simply have to act like one. You can treat it quite literally as a *role*, like in a play. There are scripts we adults memorize—etiquette books give some small idea of their variety and sophistication— and when we step out of our homes each day, the theater begins in earnest. That's not to say that there isn't acting within private spaces too, it's just different and perhaps more open to excess. Some of these excesses will come up later in this book, because what occurs behind closed doors is often way over the line of civility and even criminality, not to mention ethics.

So between knowing our roles and obeying the law, it's no problem being an adult—for the most part. Things come up, of course, whether because most adults know very little of the letter of the law—we do *not* memorize legal codes, for instance—but more often because almost all of us, at one time or another, forget the proper adult scripts. Since there are so many of them to keep straight, we often do not pass them on to teens in any systematic way. The stuff you learn in school does not help with this, as we will see in the relevant chapter later on. Adults are, in other words, simply busy being adults. And since teenagers do not have to be adults quite yet, we pass over much of the responsibility we might have to you and say to ourselves, "It can wait."

This is exactly what we say about sex. Not because sex is the private domain of adults. Not because younger people physically cannot have sex. Not because we think sex is evil, and, most importantly, not because there isn't a ton of information out there, everywhere, about it. No, it is because it is easier to 'just say no' to sex, or rather, to sex education, than to have to go over the whole thorny and horny dilemma that it seems to represent. Given this, you might wonder if it would be better to explore sex for yourselves, since adults seem to have way more hang-ups about it than you. This is, of course, an option. You are also getting a lot of mixed messages about sex. Authority figures usually condemn it. Media usually exalt it. Sex is at once cool and uncool, good and bad. Truth be known, sex is just as difficult for adults as it is for teens. We have more practice at it. This means we know the scripts better, like everything else that marks an adult role. How many people have we slept with, we might ask ourselves? For some, it is a record of infamy, for others, it is a statistic that rivals those of sports, something to be bragged about. I don't know about what women talk about when they are with other adult women. But men, if sex comes up, are happy to speak of their conquests in a manner that any fifteen-year-old would immediately recognize.

So while a reasonable rationale for teens to be cautious about sex does exist—it includes the gradual learning of the scripts and how to protect oneself against undesirable consequences—adults have been of little help. In fact, we tend to use this rationale to forbid, or severely limit, teen sexuality. Instead, what you need from us is information and maybe some compassionate stories about our own experiences at your age—if we can even recall them—that do not moralize. We don't need to be telling you "I did this and this and look what happened," or worse, "I suffered, so you will too." (*This* nasty statement, by the way, provides a common theme for much of this book.) *The good reasons for being alert about sex have nothing to do with a reason for doing it.* Like I said earlier, unlike other things, sex can be a stand-alone thing.

Easy example: it takes an average of three months of regular unprotected sex to get pregnant. There are more miscarriages then pregnancies to term, by far. Most miscarriages, also called spontaneous abortions, happen before the woman even knows she is pregnant. Because of this, we do not have solid data on how many times conception does not work out. When adults are trying to have a child, they are aware of these issues and have to really try to get pregnant. Some take it to the extreme and set up a sex schedule, which sounds like a lot of fun. But like anything, too much of the same thing makes it dull. "It's three o'clock," my wife shouts, "get up here and nail me!" All this just shows that pregnancy is not at all an inevitable outcome of sexual intercourse. And of course, there are many, many other ways of having sex than just the usual. You *could* go through your entire adolescence unprotected, engaging in non-vaginal intercourse for the most part, and escape unwanted kids. No more teen moms, which would mean a loss of profit for certain television shows.

What is really lame about all of this comes out when you get caught. The usual refrain from teens, "But we only did it once!" is met by an even greater hypocrisy on behalf of adults. Why? Because we know the odds that this statement is true are astronomically high. It would be almost like winning certain casino games. Yet our response tends to be, "Well, I told you this would happen if you had sex, and it did." In other words, it's almost a lie to say if you have sex you will make a baby. Then we compound that lie by using it again as a further device of social control. While teens are being lame in their dishonesty, adults are being manipulative in ours, and that's a lot worse.

So what's almost certainly going on is that you have been having sex for some time and you effed up, so to speak. On our part, we have been trying to manipulate you from the start, and you just gave us some big help. Better to state the facts: you're pregnant because you did not know what you were doing, forgot if you did know, or said "WTF, it won't happen." In fact, you probably already are quite aware that unprotected sex is a small risk over the short term with regard to pregnancy. It is also a small risk for disease, because most young teens have never had sex before and thus are not originally a source of disease. On the other hand, about one in three college-aged persons—mostly adults, remember, in social and chronological terms—have some kind of sexually transmitted disease. Most of these are treatable, but they are still a pain, and they do affect your health. But that only shows that teens have a lot of unprotected sex over the years.

All this is *not* a condemnation of sex. It is a critique of forced ignorance and its reaction. Adults try to forbid teen sex by using scare tactics based on false information.

Teenagers say forget it and then put themselves at risk because of the precise lack of real information and education, but also—let's admit it—because you are pissed off at us and tend to do what you want anyway. But if we gave you what you needed you would probably have less sex. Indeed, the statistics show this. In places where abstinence is preached, there are more teen pregnancies and incidents of disease. In places where there is straight-up sex ed with no moralizing—just technical stuff and maybe some techniques as well—there are less unwanted consequences.

But there is another set of reasons that adults are fond of, which have no redeeming qualities. Let's look at those. You have probably heard of resentment. It is a common enough feeling for people of all ages and types. We might feel a little resentful if someone has better grades than us and appears not to have had to study as hard, or if someone is more beautiful. Resentment is a negative feeling, but it usually passes without too much effort on the part of our conscience. We are generally taught not to envy others or be covetous. The fact that we still are speaks to our sense of unfairness. To say life isn't fair is a decoy, however, because it suggests that one can't do anything about it, when this is patently false. But more about that later on.

Since it is much easier for young people to be beautiful and sexy than older folks, according to today's general standards, we adults often feel resentment toward you. We wonder where our own youth has gone and the feelings associated with it. We do not have sex anywhere near as much as younger people, and the older we get, often the less sex there is. We are in fact jealous of you, but this alone is not the fatal problem. Jealousy in one area of life is compensated with advantages in other areas. We may not be sexy and beautiful, but we are the ones who own property, who have jobs and money, social status, solid relationships, and authority. Resentment in this kind of setting always moves over to saying "so there!" But resentment and envy can move in another direction—toward what is called 'ressentiment.' This word looks and sounds like the French for resentment, but it means more than the usual thing. 'Malicious existential envy' is often used as the definition for 'ressentiment.' This means that we do not stop at envying what you have or are, but we wish you were not alive at all. We want to trade places with you as a human being, and for this you must die. We resent, in other words, your very *existence*, and hence the word 'existential' in the definition.

This feeling is obviously malicious, even evil, because it suggests that another person should not have the right to exist. Adults can fall into this trap with regard to teenagers specifically about sex and beauty. It always has to do with our sense that we missed out on a part of our youth. We can never get it back, of course, so our resentment builds. We manifest this negative feeling by condemning or forbidding all kinds of activities, not only sex, though that is probably the biggest issue, and then label them as 'for adults only.' The source of 'adult entertainment' has nothing to do with maturity and adulthood in any *existential* sense. That is, it is not true that only adults can practice these activities. It is a way to keep young people from what are most properly the delights and pleasures of youth. We draw these lines, as we have seen, for other, more rational reasons. But we also draw and enforce them so stringently because we resent your ability to experience them so effortlessly and naively. Adults are the ones with hang-ups about sex, not teens. And the biggest reason we are so neurotic about it is because the previous generations of adults suffered upon us the same restrictions—more or less—as we are now putting on you.

This is the real result of ressentiment: we cannot outright kill most other people and replace them with ourselves. We cannot go back in time and become a beautiful and sexy teenager again—most of us were probably dorky and nerdy anyway, truth be told. So instead of this extreme and fatal action that we desire to take, we try to take much of the fun out of young people's lives. Because we also had that done to us by our parents, etc., we now have sexual hang-ups that we *project* upon you. It's in our heads, but we make sex so threatening and risky for teens that you begin to develop fears and then perhaps even anxieties about it.

If the first set of reasons should rationally tell young people to be alert and cautious about certain kinds of sex, the second set of reasons has no saving grace whatsoever. All it amounts to is older people trying to control younger people because when the former were young, they were controlled in much the same way. This control over others is the heartland of ressentiment. Someone else is controlling my life, which is tantamount to, or almost, saying that we do not deserve to have our own lives. This in turn is almost at the full step of ressentiment, which says, remember, that we do not deserve to live at all. If life is for living, then caution, education, and alertness are great. Anxiety too can be a positive force if it turns us in these other directions. But it tends to be negative because it comes from our sense that we do not know what we are doing, that we have lost control. Someone else—we adults—have taken control and we are not going to give it up to you. So our anxiety becomes your anxiety, and we can rest smugly and say that we are doing the moral thing.

Young people can and should question all of this anytime you feel that you are being controlled unreasonably. You can always tell. If there is no rational argument—if adults keep using the words 'values,' 'morals,' and calling attention to the family name or status—then you know you are being manipulated. If adults simply seem to be exercising their authority— "I forbid it because I am your parent."— call them on it. Demand a rational argument. If adults give you the facts about sex and ways you can protect yourself against the potential negative consequences of having sex, then that is what you are looking for. Nothing more, nothing less.

There is one more annoying thing about teen sexuality that comes from adults. This time, however, it is not really entirely our fault. We all know that because youth is associated with sexuality and beauty that many adults try to remain young looking and fit as long as they can. Generally this kind of health is a good idea anyway, sex aside. But in doing so, we remain not only attracted to the ideals of youth and beauty but also to the real persons who exhibit those standards. Many of these persons are not adults, and this is where the problem begins. Adult women get a break here, because young guys mature a lot more slowly than young girls. Even an eighteen-year-old guy is sometimes quite weedy looking. So adult women can lust after young men and never be seen as criminals or pedophiles. This may be a double standard, but it is unavoidable. Because girls mature beginning as young as twelve, adult men face the problem of desiring young women who are not adults but teenagers. Just check the Internet. There are hundreds of thousands of photos and videos of teenage girls naked or in otherwise sexual positions and settings. Most of this material has been hijacked from 'sexting' or has been posted by the girls themselves 'just for fun,' or to let other girls know that they are serious about their sexual sensibilities. The audience for all this, while it would include teenage boys, also includes adult men.

In general, if you are not comfortable with the idea that a bunch of old fogies are checking you out without your knowledge—it might be a lot worse if you knew, in fact—then you probably should not be creating this kind of material. Teenage boys too have an audience, which includes older gay guys and adult woman. (This is where some adult women can go over the line without exposing themselves.) The vast majority of sexual material that could be seen as pornographic because of the lack of consent from minors is of teenage girls. Indeed, if you are not a legal adult, you *cannot* legally give consent to the production and distribution of sexual material. And we are not talking about eighteen- and nineteen-year-olds either. You too are young and desirable, but all of this legal and ethical stuff is irrelevant because you can make your own decisions about whether or not you want to show off for us older folks.

That's another funny thing about very *suddenly* being an adult. Erotic sites exploit this threshold with 'barely legal' or 'eighteens' common advertising phrases. Both directions are pushed. Sites hire women who are legal adults but look younger than they are and then falsely bill them as 'jailbait.' Surveys in teen fashion magazines have regular themes about teen sex. One I recall concerned adult men on the question of, "What thing would you most like to do if you could get away with it?" The top response was, seemingly inevitably, that men would have sex with fifteen-year-old girls. Films such as *American Beauty* and *Poison Ivy* play on these desires, and the (in)famous novel *Lolita* is considered a classic.

All of this is inevitable if adults continue to desire youthful sexuality and then hypocritically condemn *actual* sex among youth. Instead of web sites for adults only, what we really need are sites for teenagers only. There girls and boys could safely help each other explore their new sexuality without the prying eyes of lustful adults. More than this, we as a society need to move away from worshipping youth. That alone would solve most of these problems. Adoring the young and then limiting them is a way of saying to them that they are not really human, that they are just objects for our pleasure and cannot have any of their own.

One final note before we move on. You might well say to me that I have said a mouthful about sex, but nothing about the other part of the chapter title. I am going to follow this pattern throughout the book, saying just a few words about what I believe to be the counterpart of the main idea of each chapter. As far as love goes, you will find that you fall in and out of love on a regular basis. You will also be in love with more than one person at once, and sometimes in life you will find that you love no one and no one loves you. I am not speaking of the love of families here, obviously, though many families might be dangerous places for young people too—but more on that later as well. This coming and going of love is how life is, and it is neither fair nor unfair. It is better to love and lose than not to love at all. We are made for love in many ways, and perhaps unlike sex, the older you get, the better love gets.

I am also going to follow this summary pattern with each of the ten chapters. I'll conclude by giving each main topic a rating out of ten based on what we discussed. You might agree or disagree with my ratings, but they are only a number, a way to encapsulate the discussion and symbolize it. Because risk-taking in sex can lead to problems, and because sex can be used as a weapon, or become an addiction, I cannot give it a perfect score. But because sex, undertaken with education, alertness, and compassion as well as passion, is a healthy and normal part of being human, heightening our experience of each other and of our bodies and feelings, I will give it an eight out of ten.

2. The Secrets of Drugs (and health)

~~~~~~

If I came across as a crimson liberal in the first chapter, I am now going to come across as an indigo conservative. This is not a political book. It is a book about social and physical reality. There is no need to label reality in a political way on the topics we are looking at together. We want to know what's what, not what somebody with a vested interest wants us to believe.

If sex is mainly good, then drugs are almost completely bad. Unlike sex, drug use does not have a stand-alone zone; if you do proscribed drugs there are always negative consequences. In fact, there are not even neutral consequences to drug use. The consequences are always bad, unlike sex and a few other activities teens are likely to be interested in. So we can't say that any amount of drug use is okay, that it has no effect, or that there are ways that you can do drugs and protect yourself from unintended or negative consequences. Even the refrain 'don't drink and drive' protects us only from the effects of inebriation while operating vehicles and not the primary health effects of alcohol on the mind and body. This is so because, unlike sex, human beings do not need drugs to evolve, experience their full potential, or solidify community and kinship bonds. In fact, drugs sabotage all of these crucial human experiences.

First, a bit of history. You may be aware of the famous case of Coca-Cola, where from about 1893 to 1907, the popular 'soft' drink contained about a six-percent solution of liquid cocaine. No wonder it was popular! The advent of the Food and Drug Administration in the United States in 1907 put an end to that. But Coke was hardly the only beverage that sold itself on pleasant, short-term effects. The era between the end of the Civil War and 1907 in the United States was one of patent medicines, almost all of which were mostly alcohol—up to ninety percent in some cases, putting moonshine to shame. They bore amusing if somewhat mysterious names like Dr. Kilger's Swamp Root, or Cooper's New Discovery. Drinking them would generally make you feel quite swampy. That large doses of alcohol masquerading under pharmaceutical prescriptions would make you feel better for a time was hardly a new discovery. This charade came to an abrupt halt with the appearance of the FDA.

But what also began around this time was the further surveillance of all kinds of substances. Banning of what are now illegal drugs began here. Opium, cocaine, and marijuana all fell under the governmental axe. Then the biggest axe came down on alcohol itself. This last ban, of course, did not last. The crime wave and subsequent black market that arose was enough to convince politicians that they should at least be part of the action. Eventually, government regained control of the liquor industry and began to make a lot of money off of it in taxes. This is especially true in Canada, where cigarettes and alcohol provide a great deal of the public tax purse, sometimes referred to as 'sin taxes.' More on this irony later on. The thing we need to note here is, one, that governments have dictated which drugs are legal and illegal, and two, this discrimination is *not* based on ill-health effects. What is it based upon?

Historically, the banning of certain substances has been associated with the perceived threat of new ethnic groups arriving in various countries. Specific drug trades were found to be part of specific groups—opium with the Chinese, marijuana with the Mexicans, and cocaine with black Americans. By 'arriving' we mean that these groups, through their historical development, were found to be in competition with whites. Therefore, banning part of their trade would hamper their social ascent, or so it was surmised. The drugs that white people favored, alcohol and cigarettes especially, remained untouched.

Alcohol was repatriated more as a political maneuver. It was a compromise of sorts. It would become legal again if government could control and tax it. The same arguments are being made today for marijuana and sometimes even for all illegal drugs: legalize, control, tax. Certainly a move like this would generate huge amounts of money for governments. In some countries, especially in Europe, certain 'soft' drugs are in fact legal and have been for some time. The problem with such an idea is that none of this bears any relation to the ill effects of the use, *any* use, of such drugs. The argument that because governments already sell bad drugs to us, so who cares, is like saying, "I did this and almost killed myself, but since I didn't, I am going to do it again."

Yes, there is a huge hypocrisy involved in drug regulation and criminalization. Insofar as proponents who favor the legalization of drugs say this, they are correct. More radically, the statement that the war on drugs is basically a war on black people or the poor in general is also often true. But none of this addresses the key issue: *drug use equals drug abuse*. Whether a substance is legal or not does not make it safe, let alone healthy. The question for adults is, why do we allow dangerous substances to be marketed to ourselves but forbid teens and children from using them? Once again, an arbitrary threshold has been set up. This boundary has nothing to do with physical reality. Drugs are just as bad for adults as they are for kids, and adults use far more of them far more often. As with many other things, we simply say that once you are an adult—remember, this happens literally overnight—you can decide for yourself what is good and what isn't good for you. Except we don't. No amount of personal decision making can make drugs good. Once again, there is no kind of use, context, or protection that allows drugs to assume even a neutral stance toward us. There may be minor exceptions to this, as when we are told to drink a glass of wine with heavy food to help digestion and the heart. Statistics of heart disease in countries where wine is favored seem to support this.

This brings up a more general issue. Everything is a substance. Everything we consume has some effect on us. We need to eat food, but we sure do not need to eat fast food. We need to drink. But we do not need to drink alcohol. We need to breathe. We sure don't need to breathe in nicotine or cannabis. The distinctions are fairly clear. The medical use of marijuana, for example, is a matter of compassion to relieve pain and not to improve health. It takes us back to the era of patent medicines, where in a society in which certain social classes of people were obsessed with prudence, even prudishness, the open consumption of alcohol and similar substances could not be tolerated. So, you could imbibe in them under the category of 'medicines.' People who suffer from horrible illnesses might use pot to ease their pain, and it may have other benefits. This usage is not an exception to the rule. The human body clearly designates what is good for it and what isn't. No government legislation, warnings, advertising, or good intentions change this. You are what you consume. The fact that we feel very differently 'under the influence' is simple evidence for this. And we might well feel relief and pleasure of a lesser degree than those suffering with terminal illness. We all have our crosses to bear. What's wrong with taking a break from them?

I once sat for three years on an advisory board for a prison and rehabilitation center in the United States. Our job was to oversee the running of the operation. How many inmates were rehabilitated? When could they be released? What were the chances and contexts for backsliding or recidivism? The motto of the prisoners was "fake it to make it." That is, convince the staff and medical people that they were ready to get out of the system. Many inmates got so good at this that we were always surprised by our 'success' rates, only to be disappointed later when the same people came shuffling through the revolving door.

A local sheriff once told me that in his county of twenty thousand persons, it was the same twenty that he always kept seeing. I used to take students to the prison to volunteer there and get some training in addictions and corrections. This was always a sight for sore eyes for those held captive within its four walls. It was very depressing, but at the same time there was a darker message that was loud and clear: if one of my students were to be alone with one of the prisoners, rape or worse was a plausible outcome.

These are people just like us, except not. Something went wrong along the way to sociality, or the ability to be normatively social, to act according to the rules even if you don't support them. The fact that prisoners were perfectly capable of learning this idea was manifest in their 'fake it to make it' motto. *We are all prisoners of society. We all fake it to make it.* It's a long road to bump into a person who supports every rule in our society. Of course, there are always those who *claim* they do, but they are faking it too.

Depending on where you want to make it, to the top of the corporate ladder or just outside the prison system, you have to become a good actor. Give the audience what it wants. We are both audience and actors. We all walk the same stage. Those who screw up their scripts end up incarcerated. So it is very important to learn the scripts well and practice a lot. This is mainly what the teenage years are for, as we saw with sex. But while sex is part of the script-learning process that turns us all into adult social beings, drugs are not. Drugs sabotage our efforts, and if we are not very good at something in the first place—anything at all—drug use makes us a lot worse. Drugs really do make a bad situation worse, in all walks of life. The most conservative Christians and the most atheistic scientists would agree on this point; it is that obvious.

The pull with drugs of all kinds, licit or illicit, is that they alter the brain chemistry so that reality slips away from us. If life sucks, we can escape it. We know that this escape is momentary. This is why we always come back for more. A lot of aspects of modern life are like this. People can have shopping or eating addictions, for example. The former get into debt, the latter get fat and unhealthy. But even the idea of addiction is only an outcome. Some drugs are physiologically addicting, like cocaine, others more psychologically so, like marijuana. The hippiesque comment that pot is not addicting must be seen in this wider light. It *is* addicting. The body might not learn to crave it, as with heroin or nicotine, but the mind does. The mind we understand as the center of thinking. If you can't think straight, life is going to get even worse. Rationality and reality are our only saviors here.

The gaining of community, often through religion, can help immensely. But it is not enough that other people's theater is convincing us to join them and act like them. We need more than their support, because *everyone* is at risk for addiction and escaping life. The key to life sucking is to change life, not our brain chemistry.

In order to do that, the first step is to avoid all substances that when ingested alter our rationality. They eff up the scripts by which we maintain our civil sociality and through which others recognize as human. The rhetoric surrounding prisoners and drug users speaks to this in a particularly harsh way. We hear these unfortunate people called animals or savages and not just losers. This is unfair, because any of us could be in their shoes.

But it does expose a general feeling that we who are faking our roles well enough to get by, believing in some of it and acting out the rest, think that if we can do it, why can't they? It's the same thing when we think about those on welfare: "I have to go to work—do you think I like it?" Or dropouts: "I'm still suffering in school, and like I really love it, WTF!" Because learning to be social really is tough, full of pitfalls and often seemingly without help, the rest of us often have little sympathy for those who seem to be taking the easy way out. But they're not. They have made it immensely harder on themselves by starting up drug use. No one, I guarantee you, in my classes, and not one of you who are reading this book, would want their lives. There is no easy way out of becoming human.

Because we cannot always rely on our fellow humans for help, and because human knowledge, though vastly advanced over previous centuries, is still quite limited, we seek other sources for aid. Religion can be addicting and provide an escape from life's hardships. But religion, if it is not mere ritual, provides solid help for human beings because it is a community-making agent. Drugs always isolate. There is no religion of one. Civic voluntarism is also a way in which one can get out of oneself. By helping others we help ourselves. These others tend not to be using us. They really do need our help.

It also gives us some healthy perspective on what our lives might be like if we had grown up in even worse circumstances. The old saying, "There's always someone worse off than you," is quite true. Just don't use it to rationalize negative stuff in your own life. Canadians, for example, love to do this by comparing themselves to Americans in terms of quality of life. Canada is regularly about number five to seven on the world country list in terms of best places to live. The USA is about twenty-two or so. So Canada always looks a lot better than it actually is if it is only compared to a country that has more challenges. Australia is a more fair comparison, and last year it ranked one higher than Canada. But you never hear of that comparison up here. I wonder why?

Here's more crappy stuff about drugs. By using illicit drugs you are supporting criminals. These are usually people who are running a business. Yes, the idea of business is much the same as legal businesses, but the people who run them are not quite the same. They tend to be antisocial and amoral, as long as this word is taken in the normative sense where morality is representative of the usual rules. They would not make reliable friends. You would find it difficult to trust them. They do not play by the rules, and they do not respect those who do.

Once again, many of the rules *do* suck. But for a society to mature, all of its members have to come together and agree on what changes should be made. One group cannot opt out, for better or worse, criminal or, for another kind of instance, Amish. Such people turn their backs on the rest of us and then judge us for not living like them. Indeed, one easy thing about criminals is that they are content to have the rest of us conform, because if we didn't, it would mean more competition for them. Why would we want to support those whom we could never trust to support us?

Something similar exists on the legal side of drugs and drug use. Large corporations make huge profits on our licit drug use, like alcohol and nicotine, but also pharmaceuticals, which are often the drug of choice among the elderly and, not surprisingly, among health care professionals. The stuff is readily at hand. Governments, as we have already seen, make large amounts of taxes off tobacco and alcohol, not to mention all the sales taxes of sundry items and drugs that you can buy over the counter. In other words, the drug trade is not only criminal. In fact, we might be closing in on some kind of truth if we said that governments and licit organizations make war upon illegal drug traders because they're worried about competition. This makes sense at an individual level if someone says to you, "I prefer pot over alcohol," or "Heroin is my drug of choice; it sure beats nicotine."

Every person who abuses illegal drugs is potentially one less person who abuses the legal ones. Of course, to have a monopoly on drugs would be the ideal in this kind of system. Some governments have accused other countries of being a pusher or a pimp, depending on if certain drugs or prostitution has been legalized. This would seem to be mere rhetoric. The argument that legalizing all drugs would cut crime is reasonable. But it does not address the issue of having what are to become legal ministries, both public and private sector, becoming the drug traders. *Legalization does not alter the fact that drugs are bad.*

We hear that the illegal drug trade is worth many billions of dollars a year. People without other serious employment opportunities get involved in it at all levels. It is as much a rural phenomena as an urban one, as much white as black, Asian as Latin, male or female. Crack in the 'hood,' 'meth' on the farms. Coke parties in Manhattan, 'street smack' in The Bronx. All of this is so old hat that when you sit through drug education stuff in your schools most of you likely fall asleep. The same old warnings are worthless. Society needs to provide a cure through finding something else for people, young and old, to do that gives them a fulfilling life. Most types of work sure ain't it, so what are the options?

Well, pharmaceutical companies also make billions of dollars a year. People also get involved with them at all levels. The key is to ask what kinds of people? Remember that we are all faking it in order to make it. Making it means being available to be hired into a licit organization, for profit or not. Whatever we think of the hypocrisies of such a system of options, the only way to change it is from the inside. You cannot make real change in the world by being a bystander, and certainly nothing is going to come of addiction, whatever its flavor.

We often make an error when we think that the hordes of people who make revolutions are outsiders. No. Their numbers are a sign that they are in fact the dominant ones. Most people believe what they say. It is the elites that cling to power who do not know what a fragile hold they have on society. They make the official rules, but no one is paying attention. The rate of drug abuse has not changed much over the generations. This is another favorite lie of adults. Each younger generation is accused of promoting an explosion of drugs. It may even become a source of perverse pride, as with some of your parents, the hippies and boomers. I recently saw a pro-pot T-shirt. The wearer was not some teenager with long hair and a bad attitude. It was someone pushing seventy with little hair and getting into an expensive SUV. This fellow, among millions of others of his age group, had faked it to make it rather well. These adults have carved out an elite space in society in part to keep doing what they were doing as kids. Nice message for teens, I thought. Join the system in public and then leave it in private.

This kind of behavior is also counterproductive. To make serious change in a world where injustice and evil dwell, you can't conform all day and then escape at night. The energy that drug abuse and addiction take from the person, both physically and mentally, ensures that the world will keep rolling along as it always has. *Drugs are anti-revolutionary*, so much so that it would be fitting if our most conservative citizens promoted them!

All the teenage rebellion you will feel during these years and perhaps long after gets drained away into nothing if you use drugs. Rather, you need to focus these energies into real critique and not use them to procure some lame means of escape. Most teenagers' lives are at least bearable. It is a phase of life, and not your whole life. We will come back to this point later on when we talk about school and its negative effects on young people. For now, what may be intolerable to you can only be made worse by using drugs.

Forget our hypocritical indictment of them. Drugs keep society the way it is. Adults who realize this and do not make war on all drug abuse simply double their hypocrisy. Drug use does not challenge the system; it promotes it. In the same way, criminal organizations are just capitalists with the wrong attitude. Their goals and most of their means are the same as legal companies and governments. Because they have far less force at their disposal than do their main competitors, criminals almost always lose in direct confrontations with the legal system and its forces.

Indeed, governments, when they care to do so, often have to reign in legal corporations who are always tempted to use criminal means to get what they want. And really, is the stock market more moral than the Mafia? The former causes far more problems for far more people. Criminal organizations tend to leave regular people alone. It's way too much trouble and hurts business to cause collateral damage. Think about the difference between the conflicts among gangs versus those among nations. Gang warfare leaves dozens dead; real war leaves millions.

No, we cannot use the usual arguments to dissuade you of drug use, dealing, making, or promoting. The reality is that people lack fulfilling choices in their lives. This includes most of us. If adults provide the compassionate and caring environment kids need to become adults, drug use among the young would abruptly halt. Even if you go on to a boring job, the care from your family and others that should be there will remind you that you are too important a person to mess up with drugs.

Many teens today think they are revolutionaries. Another secret—all generations have felt this way. Some of these groups have even participated in real revolutions. But the historical facts are these: world-changing events have their sources in adults who have suffered and worked in systems they abhor for years. They muster up some support from energetic youth, but youth is never the architect of anything. This is so not merely because we keep you down, but because of your lack of experience of the wider reality; your lack of perspective does not allow the fullest meaning to come to your rebellious feelings. This is the difference between real revolution and mere rebellion. Revolution carries the meaning of discontent to its farthest point. Rebellion always stops short of this simply because it does not know what to do next.

In terms of our chapter's theme, licit drugs often aid the system. Nicotine keeps people calm and alert so they can work better. Narcotics screw up the ability to work. This is not the whole story, of course, because alcohol is generally bad for the working life, although liquid lunches can aid staff chemistry and keep people relaxed instead of in each other's faces. Sometimes, though, illicit drugs can also aid capitalism. One of the reasons why local companies aren't often too worried about rural methamphetamine use is that it produces very energetic workers. How many times have I heard when I lived in the heartland my own students telling me, "I worked a triple shift, no problem." How so? They had been doing meth ahead of time and came to work as wired as can be. Either way, whatever your drug of choice may be, the options, once you use, are either to support the system as it is and contribute to it without any hope of change, or to escape from it and be able to do nothing against it.

Drugs are not the source of anything in themselves. Drug use and addiction are always epiphenomenal, that is, they always start in response to something else. If you are being abused by your parents or relations, for example, this would be more of a *source* of potential addiction in our sense. If you go without work for years when you get a little older, this kind of thing would also be a very common potential source. Addictions of all kinds are a person's response to stress. We want to ease it, escape from it, no matter for how short a time. Life is so bad we cannot bear it. But as we said before, drug use just makes things worse, a lot worse.

The unemployed person uses all his money for drugs and eventually might starve to death on the street. The abuse victim stays in the place of abuse and escapes only in her mind for a few hours a day. All of this too is old hat. What is needed is serious support for young people so that addictions do not develop. Moralizing about it does not do anything. For adults, the situation is the same, with the exception that there is often less help available because we are supposed to be able to look after ourselves. But the fact that some cannot is a sure sign that they have not had the opportunity to develop into complete adulthood.

This partial adulthood in fact hampers all of our mutual abilities to make a good society. In the same way, it sabotages our personal relationships. We set up poor role models for our children, and you folks have every right to disbelieve everything we might say about drugs if we ourselves do not hold the line in reality. You might well feel that drug use is just another way adults make teens and others suffer.

By sending mixed messages, by moralizing without serious help, by marketing certain drugs that are often as harmful to health as the worst of the illegal ones, by selectively cracking down on the drug trades of non-whites and leaving whites relatively alone, all of this gives teens no honest answers.

You can help us by constantly reminding us that *we* are at fault with regard to drugs. By setting yourselves up as honest role models and putting us to shame, teens can eventually cure themselves of the problems associated with drugs. It might take several generations of this new attitude, but it is one that teens are already equipped to use. *Rebel against the hypocrisies and pathetic dishonesties of drug use. You have nothing to lose but your chemical chains. You have a world to win.*

Given all of this, one might think non-medical drugs would get a big fat zero. But since there is some evidence that some illicit drugs can be used for compassionate health reasons, that wine in moderation aids the body's health, and that some parents might need a stiff drink instead of beating their kids, I will give drugs a one out of ten.

3. The Secrets of 'Discipline' (and authority)

~~~~~~

Sex. Drugs. In a less serious book this chapter would be about rock and roll. But we need to stay disciplined and move on. This chapter is about just that: how to *become* disciplined about living without *being* disciplined; how to move on from the stress of social control and yet remain in control of yourself. It is a big challenge, especially in those regions where the law is on the side of a certain kind of authority. Until you reach legal age, you are more or less at the mercy of the adults around you.

Let's talk about kinds of authority first. Until the 1930s, the very word 'authority' had either a positive meaning or at least a neutral one. Thinkers interested in politics invented a new word to try to explain the rise of fascism in Europe at the time. Italy, Germany, Spain, Rumania, and Bulgaria all fell victim to an especially strict and obsessive form of politics that focused on social control. These regimes were called authoritarian. Now this is a word we are very used to today. It is used to describe basically the same thing in interpersonal relations. And it is used to describe political dictatorships of various kinds, such as in contemporary Iran or China. Authoritarian relations represent one kind of authority and not every kind. Before the 1930s, authority tended to mean 'authoritative.' This is a word you don't hear used as much today. Authoritative simply means having the rational backup for having an opinion. As a social philosopher, I would be considered to have some authoritative weight in certain areas because I have studied and written about them. But since I am not a dictator, nor do I have any real power over others, I could not be said to be able to be an authoritarian.

Authority then is a much-abused word. One of the mottos of your parents was 'Question authority.' They of course were brought up in the post-war period of increasing social control, and they quite rightly reacted against it. Before turning away through drug use and other popular culture fantasies, they had an inkling of what the world might be like if people let each other live and let live. Ironically, by the 1980s, these same persons were very much over on the other side of things. They became supporters of authority in the stricter sense, and it is you who are now paying for that change.

A good question for your parents and teachers, especially the older ones, is, "What on earth were you thinking of?" When authority figures question your actions, come right back and question theirs. If they have a reasonable explanation, one that takes account of real historical events and their biographical experience, then they may be on their way to an 'authoritative' account of their demands on you. If not, then continue to question them.

Why do I say this at the beginning of the chapter? *Because societies where the ability to question is lost or given away become like the Nazis.* They become authoritarian. They obsess about social control and are interested in very little else. Whether at the level of society or the individual, the effect of authoritarian styles of discipline and control is always the same. I command; you obey. Rules are always interpreted in the strictest, most literal sense, akin to how some people interpret religious texts like the Bible. People who get hooked into authoritarian relationships are open for abuse. Rules are laid down and strictly adhered to without bending them to take into consideration the always differing contexts into which people fall. The rules appear as if they are timeless and descended from God. It is understandable historically why religious persons think that way. Thousands of years of similar interpretations might be hard to shrug off overnight. But when other kinds of people and institutions adopt these older manners of rule-reading and rule-following, the abuses immediately begin to pile up.

Words begin to take on new meanings. As with 'authority,' 'discipline' becomes something that is experienced as harsh and unforgiving. Authority actually means a number of different things, and it is a fair question to ask, "What kind of authority are we talking about?" Same with discipline. It used to simply mean an ability to habitually and perhaps ritually perform certain activities. There was a discipline of prayer for those who lived in monasteries, for instance. Today this kind of meaning might well apply to the discipline of the ballet student. Then it took on a more recent meaning. The sciences and arts became known as different 'disciplines,' a meaning they still carry today in the universities.

It takes a slightly different kind of disciplinary knowledge and skill to excel in the different sciences. Someone who is good at math might not be good at art, that sort of thing. Each discipline requires of us a different knack and set of habits. Some favor organizational skills and memory, others more spontaneity and creative thinking. It is absolutely *not* the case that discipline just means structured activity and thinking. The discipline of the artist may appear to be more chaotic than that of the mathematician, but each is necessary to its own device.

But more recently with the rise of modern nations and especially with the Nazis in the twentieth century, discipline took on a more ominous tone. It came to be associated with strict social control, especially over children and adult workers. Social relations in the family and the workplace became more militaristic. You needed to obey without question. For thousands of years, really since the beginning of farming, social groups disciplined their children in a way that many today would consider severe. But the idea in ancient times was that such discipline was a means to the end of making children into adults. Today, thanks to the politics of fascism, which *every state in the world partakes in to some extent,* discipline has become an end in itself. To be disciplined is the goal. There is no other implication or value.

The general idea is that if one becomes disciplined, one can turn to anything and be successful in it. With ballet as a foundation, for example, a dancer can master other styles of dance all the more easily. But the discipline of an art like dance is not severe, harsh, or part of a sadistic ritual. It simply is disciplined in that it is habitual, focused, and alert. So the kind of discipline that you should always question is like the kind of authority that you should always question. Any time an adult simply tries to discipline you by fiat, which means by virtue only of the social status and power they have over you, you should resist in the best way you can.

The best form of resistance to authoritarian discipline is to play by the rules publicly and not internalize the rules privately. That is, be the best teenager you can be in terms of what these dangerous adults expect of you, but never let their actual ideas sink into your head. If certain adults cannot be reasoned with, then don't try.

Authoritarians are always spoiling for a fight. They are both bullies and cowards. They know they can have their way with you through corporal punishment or other forms of discipline, and sometimes the law is on their side. Such people live to exert control over others. If they cannot do so in their public lives, like at work or church, they will inevitably seek to do so in the privacy of their homes. They become like little dictators. Often it is the father figure who assumes this role, but not always. It can be both parents, one or the other, some teachers and school administrators, and not others, entire school districts, certain churches, and not others. You get the picture. If the wider society in your region supports this kind of violence against children, sometimes with physical and sexual abuse, all you can do is avoid it.

If the laws favor kids and teenagers, as they do for some contexts in Canada and other countries, then take full advantage of the law by contacting social service ministries, the police, or health care professionals. There are often hotlines set up in communities to help children. Teenagers should not be ashamed to use them. Don't be cowed by an adult's anger. Let them know that you will defend yourself.

Don't get me wrong, either. I know I would be sorely tempted to do the wrong thing with certain young people because teenagers can be really annoying sometimes. But no matter how I *feel* as an adult, disciplining minors in the authoritarian way we are speaking about in this chapter is the wrong thing to do. Let's take a look at some of the reasons.

It sounds like I am telling you to grin and bear it. The disconcerting thing in these places where discipline is thought of as violent and fascist is that it is not thought of as extreme. It remains the norm, like in the Southeastern United States and Texas, for example. People almost come across as enjoying hitting their kids down there! At the very least, they are shameless about it. "Kids need to learn discipline," is the refrain. "We can't just let 'em run wild." A recent video posting on You Tube of a sixteen-year-old girl being whipped by her father using a large leather belt demonstrates the horror of this kind of setting. It is disgusting all the more as the father—ironically and disconcertingly a family-court judge in Texas—in an interview suggested that he was not only within his rights, but that it was *the right thing to do*. It is *this* that is the key.

When people truly believe that what they are doing is right, the law is something extraneous. People do not generally act the way they do just because a law tells them to. We are not that disinterested in our own feelings and in our traditions. It is rather customs that guide our actions. And if it is normal to whip your kids until they turn eighteen, then that is exactly what is going to happen. Even if the law does not support it, as it does not in most developed countries, that law still has to be *enacted* if the social norms are the other way. Since none of you asked to be born into these contexts, we can immediately say, "watch your back!"

But we can offer more than that. If you have authoritarian parents, listen to their demands and try to figure out if they have rational reasons for telling you to do this and not do that. You can use history as a guide here. When culture heroes like Moses, say, come back to their group with a new set of rules that claim to be God-given, these rules are usually concise statements of what the culture ideally believes anyway. "Thou shalt not kill" applies evenly within any culture. No society can afford to have its members killing each other off. Of course, we abandon the wider meaning of this commandment when we kill those of other cultures. But the commandment was never meant to be taken in the wider sense. The Christians later reinterpreted this statement and attempted to extend it to all humans. That this has had limited success is obvious.

Try the same logic in your home or school. In these small places, you know the rules and the consequences. Often they are absolutely trivial and have only to do with the exercise of power and control, like you will be 'spanked' if you miss your curfew, or if you get a note sent home from school, or something less extreme but still unfair will happen to you. I put the word 'spank' in quotes because like authority and discipline, this word too has taken on a new and ominously false meaning. School administrators speak of 'spanking' a teen with a paddle. Uh, that's not spanking. Parents speak of 'spanking' their kid with a strap. Right. You know what I am saying here. Not that spanking in the older sense, with the adult's hand as the only weapon, is reasonable either, but at least it might feel a little less like an out and out assault. And spanking in this sense really does hurt the adult too. It's hard on the hand! But if this is the way in which you are growing up, take it like you take history. Outside of this little world the rules are different. When you become an adult you are free of these punishments and rules.

In these small places, small thinking is the ultimate guide and rule. You have to enlarge your own thinking and you may have to do it without a lot of help. Your friends may have this same challenge, but they may be scared to engage in it. So might you. Nevertheless, if you don't want to fall victim to abuse later in life, if you don't want to become like your parents and abuse your own kids, you need to carve out a private space for thinking in a wider sense.

Just like the Christians tried to do with the idea of killing, you need to extend the spirit of the word discipline and lose its letter. By this I mean you need to take on the responsibility for your own self-control and never let it be given away to others. If you do give it away, you will lose the power of decision and eventually thought itself. You will become both an abuser and a victim of abuse. The *spirit* of discipline is that you are focused, alert, and conscious of what you want and need in life. You are organized in the specific manner you need to be for whatever work and interests you follow. The *letter* of discipline is what you might have grown up with: punishments of unreasonable variety and severity; rituals that were both theatrical and sadistic—bend over, young lady—that sort of thing. You might have begun to suspect that it was your parents or other adults who actually lacked self-control. What adult maintains authentic control and authority and feels the need to hit his or her kids?

This is the next point I want to talk about with you. It is correct to say that the person who calls upon his authority has already lost it. If an adult says to you that you must do something because they said so, or because they are so and so and you are only you, that means they have no real authority over you. They are calling attention to their official status because you have already exposed them for what they are—bullies and cowards. If we see authority and respect it because we respect the values it represents—the authority of science or religion, for example—then we obey because we want to. We think obeying is *good in itself*. If we obey, we receive the goods of authority. We in fact can become part of the very authority we are obeying. This might even feel good. Not only because adults will leave you alone. It feels good because whatever values are at stake are becoming your values. Values are not beaten into teenagers. They take shape in your mind because they demonstrate themselves in the real world. They demonstrate that they work. Like not killing. Like not assaulting people. Like not bullying. Like not trying to control other people for the sake of self-interest. This is what we can call authentic authority. It reminds us of the older meaning of the word—the word 'authoritative,' the one we don't hear used too much today. It got lost in the battle over 'questioning authority' and the authority adults might have to discipline you. The only legitimate use of authority comes from the knowledge and experience of consequences. Science, although it can proclaim a religious-like authority, is, at its best, an anti-authority tool. Its methods ideally state that arguments from authority are worthless. What does this mean? It is evidently talking about *both* authoritarian and authoritative forms of authority. But how is it possible to not have any authority at all?

Science learns by experiment and experience. But there is always the next experiment, the next experience. So science seeks a balance between what has been the case and what may be the case. In other words, science is aware of what has occurred in the past but does not offer it any undue respect. The present context is what matters. And the present is always opened up by the future. What do I mean by this? The future is, by definition, an open book. Nothing is for certain. All we know is that things will change in some manner, large or small. Of course we can suggest the likelihood of specific outcomes. The weather forecast is a common example of this. But the future does not dictate to us in the way the past tries to. It is we who turn the page. We are often surprised by what we see when we turn it. The sense that we cannot know what is going to happen may give us anxiety, as when we are dreading outcomes that we think are likely but which we have not yet actually experienced. If we have been in a similar situation before and something bad happened, we might well think that we are going to repeat the mistake or the bad experience. The fact that we think we know how things will turn out can also give us anxiety. So there is an odd paradox about living only in the present, which is all we can do. We want to know about what is going to happen to us, and we also sometimes don't want to know. Expectations are okay if you keep them modest. We strive to avoid disappointment. We seek control over our lives.

This is where the argument from authority comes in. It acts like it can save us from uncertainties of all kinds. Parents, teachers, gods, history, technology, governments, even science itself can play this role. But it is a disingenuous role. By this I mean the people involved themselves are unsure of things and are seeking control over others—yourselves. The sense of falseness, of their being motivated by something other than what they are telling you is what makes the role of authority disingenuous. Arguments from experience and experiment are what the ideal scientist is saying should replace arguments from authority. Yet experience and experiment generate their own form of authority. It may be future-oriented and thus open-ended, but it still has the power to sway us. This contextual authority puts limits on what it can tell us to do and how it wants us to act. It is authority *for the time being* only. It can be altered. It can be mistaken. It is this kind of authority I am going to recommend to you to listen to and try to construct with the adults around you.

So if you approach authority figures in your life with the sense that you are willing to consider past experience in your future actions and decisions, then together you can weigh the results of these previous events and take them into consideration when you are making future plans. Let's say last time you went on a date your significant other got pulled over for speeding—a common occurrence when teens get into cars together. (Interestingly, but perhaps not surprisingly, when teens drive alone, they rarely break the law.) Both sets of parents were pissed. Things escalated and your parents told you that you were not allowed to even see this other person again except at school. This was an outcome you would not have expected even when you saw the flashing police car lights. On the other hand, you know your parents. They can be temperamental. They might even lash out once in a while. While some parents use punitive discipline as a matter of course, most parents who either hit their kids or impose grossly unreasonable sanctions or punishments upon them do so because they are reacting in the moment. They're angry, and they are going to take it out on what they believe is the source of their anger—you. But most often for these kinds of parents they are actually reacting to something else. Mine were no different, though they never actually hit me. For my parents, it was always anxiety over work and money, and maybe some other stuff to which I was never privy.

In their moment of frustration, they exert the authority of status over you. Simply because they are your parents is argument enough.

But in fact, that is no argument. Remember, arguments from authority are worthless in this sense. The problem here is not merely the absence of rationality, but the presence of *betrayal*. We feel, as adults, that you, as teens, have betrayed us. This sounds really serious and over the top. What I mean is that the kid they love has done something to add to their troubles. Ideally, people whom we love never betray us but only help us get over our problems. Humans must do this together or usually not at all. Look at it another way. Adults speed all the time. Most of us are not pulled over because we are either more clever about when we do it, or we drive vehicles that the police slack off on. It is well known that 'Mom's taxi' is the vehicle that per capita speeds the most. It is almost never pulled over because not only are these women the same as the wives of the male police officers, everyone cuts them a break because they see themselves, their own families, as involved in the same thing. But if it's a sixteen-year-old (especially) male driving a red coupe, then watch out. You are going get nailed at some point. There are even insurance company tables about what to charge depending on not only the type of vehicle, and obviously the age of the driver, but also the vehicle color! The police are the bull, and your red car the flag.

So your punishment of missing your mate has nothing to do with your actual actions. It is simply about the fact that your error has hurt your parents in a much deeper way. You have betrayed them and hurt their feelings. You are supposed to love and be loyal to them, and you somehow forgot that. This is inevitable, of course, especially when it comes to teen romance, where your feelings are turning away from your family and to your peers in powerful ways. This is also a necessary experience in growing up, and we adults rationally cannot resent it. But love, loyalty, friendship, and family are not always rational. Their forbidding you to see the one you love hurts deeply. Your parents have done that on purpose because they feel as if you have hurt them just as deeply. Speeding is irrelevant to any of this. It could have been anything.

All of this is commonplace. Hopefully, over a few days or weeks, the authority figures in your life back off and recant some of their anger. They allow you and your mate to get together again. Maybe not in a car at night, but that does not really matter. Hurt feelings are gotten over, and things return to normal until the next time. If you want to avoid a next time, *take notes*—literally—on your past experiences and consult them regularly. Treat growing into an adult the way you are forced to treat school. It's an easy tool and anyone can do it, no matter what age you are or what experiences you have had. You could make two books. A black one for the mistakes and the negative consequences, a green one for all the times when life was a 'go,' when you and your parents had a great time, or even a neutral one, and they gave you positive consequences.

That horrifying video I mentioned earlier, with the father who whipped his sixteen-year-old daughter for apparently looking at the Internet when he had told her not to, wow— how petty and trivial can you get? But I can guarantee you something else was at the back of it, and whatever it might have been was likely not anything to do with the teen or the net. Ironically, the full video on YouTube was classified as adult viewing only. However scary, you teens need to be able to see it. Not as a cautionary tale, but more to give you a sense that in extreme situations adults can basically lose their perspective. We can still act as if we were angry kids, which is not to excuse the adult in this case or any other case even remotely like it. But this is a simple fact: being an adult means taking on the stresses of the world. We find, inevitably, that there are things we cannot control in the wider world and in our lives—many things. Sometimes the one thing it seems we can control is our kids. But with teens, that control goes out the window enough times to not merely make us angry but give us a sense of desperation, and even worse, *alienation*. What is this? Being alienated means feeling that whatever you do, nothing is going to come of it. It is a very dangerous feeling. You literally feel like an alien, that is, your humanity begins to slip away. Unless the adult is a true sadist—more on that in a second—when we act out in violence and anger toward you as our children, we are ultimately experiencing alienation. The betrayal we feel from you—even though this was almost never your intent— pushes us away from the social relationships we rely on to maintain our own humanity. We are desperate enough to do anything to force the situation back into what it was before the error occurred. We might even imagine tying you to a chair in the basement if we could get away with it. We realize, as parents, and perhaps in other authority roles, that we have no authority at all unless there is someone there to listen to our demands. It may well be that in our post-farming society, where labor is not needed as it was in the past, that people have kids just to feel less alienated. Nothing else in modern public life can be as fulfilling as having a family.

So when you start to move away from the authority of family and school and toward other kinds of more anonymous authority structures, like work and the legal system, we feel hurt. Most of us know deep down it has to be this way. Our hurt feelings speak, most positively, to our love for you. We're going to miss you, and we can't deny it. We also feel guilty. We cannot be sure you are going to miss us. We know we've made mistakes. We know we've hurt you. We might even say to ourselves, "If I were my kid, I would not see me for years." This is sad, but common enough. We brought you into this world, or adopted you from a worse world into a better one, because of our need for human community and because the wider world seldom produces that kind of community on its own. Religion may be one exception, but more on that in its own chapter.

For you to become an adult—which *is* what almost all of us want, after all—you have to break down this community and then reconstruct it. It is always a painful and trying experience for both adults and teenagers. Neither side really knows what it is doing, because these are simply new experiences.

The limits of authority and discipline are often exposed in times of crisis. We can treat you as punitively as we want under the relevant laws, but this usually results in kids actually not seeing their parents again, and rightly so. We can treat you with respect and love and you will still betray us. As adults, we just have to get over that and move on. Because we are more experienced and more mature, we are supposed to be able to do that without causing you too much harm. There are cases, of course, where we don't. Avoid the sources of these moments that are under your control at all costs. Go for a walk instead of a drive, for instance, to come back to our hypothetical scenario, if you think your mate is going to have to show off. There are other ways of impressing your partner. Honesty and maturity are some of the best.

Aside from note-taking for yourself, which all teens and adults could do in family situations, you should read each other's notes. See how your parents feel about you and share your feelings about them with them. Communication during normal times cuts the amount of crisis time way down. Even rationally oriented and practical adults have pet peeves. These may have no serious basis. You cannot have a peeve against drug use, for instance, because drugs really are a negative thing objectively. But pet peeves are idiosyncratic and unreasonable. Internet time could be one. How much time you spend on the Internet does not matter, but some adults imagine it does, so you may have to negotiate it. In your negotiation, don't stop questioning the disingenuous authority that makes petty demands of you. Don't let the authority figures just have it their way—just because. Make them present a serious and rational argument. Most of us, when pushed, can do that. When we cannot, it tells you that what you want to do is actually *not* a big deal.

But, there are contexts and families where this may be dangerous, like the kind that was exposed by the Texas teen's home video. If you think or know that you are in *that* kind of context, be very cautious about confrontation. Like I said before, you can obey the local rules and know that you will shortly be free of them when you turn eighteen or graduate from high school. Move out as soon as you can, because while the law *now* protects you, you still have to enact it. And then you almost always end up in a 'he said, she said' situation where the law and its forces have trouble acting. Indeed, even where there are laws protecting teens and children from violence and abuse—and I mean all those that hide under the disingenuous masks of 'discipline' and 'authority'— these are not always enforced. Such laws are hard to enforce because a lot of bad stuff happens behind closed doors. Take a walk through any middle-class suburb and allow yourself to wonder what is going on inside those neat and cozy houses. You don't want to know, perhaps. But in fact, you *do* already know. But who listens to teenagers anyway?

We know that ninety-five percent of sexual and physical abuse happens to kids from relatives, usually close ones. This is just the stuff that gets reported. Like the drug trade, the amount that gets caught is low compared with the amount actually going on.

I am going to lay it on heavy here. One of the dirtiest of the big secrets is that many adults try to rationalize abuse by imagining it is discipline, and some adults even enjoy doing so. These latter are real sadists, and they do exist. 'Spanking' has been cited as a form of not only physical abuse but sexual as well, especially if adults have the ritual practice of hitting you when you are partially or fully unclothed. Remember, the word 'spanking' has been altered to cover for all kinds of corporal punishment, no matter how dangerous and severe. For example, in about twenty US states, hitting kids with heavy pieces of wood—' paddles' is their euphemism—is still lawful in schools. In the home you can do far worse. Remember that because it is legal it generally means most adults in those regions support it. This is the truly sobering issue. Do adults in those locales hate their kids?

Probably not. It's probably the same amount as in any other region. Often such punishment comes from parents who did not really want to be parents and who take it out on their innocent children. But what I am saying is not about this or that adult hating this or that kid or teen. It is about a system that sees you as not fully human, without full human rights, and sees that it is right to abuse you simply because you are you. *This* is the truly scary thing about so-called discipline, physical or otherwise.

Adults run into each other and are annoyed and angered almost every day. But we can't assault each other because it is illegal and because we know we are not supposed to treat other people like that. All this goes out the window sometimes with teenagers. Teens know very well how annoying they can be. You are not innocent like an infant. You don't always try your best. You aren't always honest. You don't always care about us. So what? We know that, too. *And, yes, we feel the same way about you.*

The problem isn't that we can't get along if we work at it. It is that we have too high expectations of each other. We idealize family life way too much. When it does not meet our inflated expectations, we get disappointed, perhaps resentful and angry, and even irrational and dangerous. We need to back off and say sometimes, "It's just a family." Even easier, "It's just school. It's just teens. It's just adults. It's just life."

We need to get a life, all of us adults, if we find ourselves becoming too obsessed with controlling and disciplining you folks. *You* need to get a life—well, that *is* what you are trying to do as a teen, is it not?— if you think that we are here only to serve you and always put you first.

Teens don't need discipline in the new and negative sense. Assaulting others is illegal unless you have a very strong sense you are defending yourself against certain injury or death. Assaulting people who are smaller than us is cowardly. Enjoying it is sadistic. I mention this again because a perennially popular erotic kink as evidenced on the net and elsewhere is about corporal punishment and 'discipline.' Very often legal adults are pretending that they are kids or teens. But it is a sure sign that sadism is out there and may be a factor in your home. Some of the Nazis were trained to be sadists. They enjoyed what they were doing as well as feeling it was the right thing to do. Some adults may be hiding their enjoyment under the mask of thinking 'disciplining' is the right thing to do. 'Spanking' etc. is a very real part of this equation. For some adults, *it is a legally sanctioned way of having indirect sex with their kids or someone else's*, depending on their social role. Wow, another big dirty secret. I am not saying this is common, but it is real. It is something to think about ahead of time and avoid. Don't be scared of it, but be alert to its possibility. We need to know what's what.

Because discipline can be a good thing in specific contexts, like ballet or law school or in the sciences, and because the authority of experience is a necessary tool we all must use to step into the future, and because self-discipline is a sign of maturity, we cannot completely say that discipline is bad. But because most uses of discipline are negative, perhaps punitive, and some even sadistic, because its main goal seems to be the social control of teenagers and others, and because it demands that you obey the fake authority of either unreasoned tradition, habit, ritual, or social status, I am going to rate discipline a three out of ten.

4. The Secrets of School (and learning)

〰〰〰〰〰〰〰〰〰〰〰〰〰〰〰〰〰〰〰〰〰〰〰〰

After a chapter like that, who wants to talk about school? My apologies, but we need to 'go to school on school.' That's right. We need to study school in the way school demands we study the stuff it pushes on us. That's what we are going to do together in this chapter.

School is first of all a warehouse. If you think about just how much time school takes up in your life, from ages four to eighteen and beyond, I think you'll agree that it is one of the ten things where some other big secrets are held. Since you are in school up to eight hours a day, maybe far more if you are involved in other activities, you're in the warehouse for most of your waking hours. If you add in homework, which is first and foremost a device to extend the school day and a method of surveillance where you can be watched without any watchers, the warehouse gets larger and larger.

Adults need a place to store kids while the kids are growing up. This is especially the case for teenagers. This is because the older you get without yet reaching the chronological or official age of adulthood, the more trouble you can get into. School takes way more time than it needs to. There have been famous reports that the amount of actual stuff you learn could be concisely taught in about a hundred hours, some say a hundred days. Whatever the actual time is—people aren't just guessing on this, they've done the experiments—fourteen years plus added hours 'out' of school isn't it. There is another reason you are in school for so effing long, and it's because you are a nuisance.

And because *we* had to do it. Once again, notice the same old dreary logic that forces you to do things we want you to do. We suffered, so you must suffer, and on and on down the generations. It is fair to say that many children in the world suffer less than did their ancestors. But the slow progress toward treating you like human beings is often artificial. The system as a whole needs schools to stay the way they are. This is because their other chief function, aside from warehousing annoying kids and even more annoying teens, is to shape you into passive producers and consumers.

Even the mighty media cannot do this by itself. All the advertising in the world is not going to make a human into a consumer. And *if marketing makes the consumer, school makes the producer.* You have to *learn to earn.* Learning to earn is the key to all learning in our current educational system. It does not matter if you're not into it. What you say is irrelevant, as I am sure most of you have already noticed about being in school.

Oh, the rationalizations are many and diverse. Kids don't know what they need to know, which is true insofar as they have not learned the basic literacies of mathematics, science, language, and history. So what? How many adults can tell you what they learned in high school? And how relevant to their adult lives is much of what they did learn? The fact that they cannot recall most of it is *all* the evidence we need. *People remember what they need to know.* No more, no less. I probably could not pass a high school math class. But, to be fair, I do need the basic math skills to know what is going on with our household budget, taxes, salary, retirement, and the like. How long would it take to learn that bit?

What about kids not having the maturity to control their own destinies? Well, most kids and teens I have met don't seem to be in need of controlling much of anything, let alone other people. You guys do that mainly because you're thrown together simply because you live in the same neighborhood and not because you are friends. This togetherness is of course not random. You likely come from similar social classes and statuses, borrowed from what your parents are and what they do. Our cities are arranged that way. Rich people live with other rich people, the poor with themselves. But this is not enough to ensure conformity that the school demands of you. You force each other to conform through rumor, gossip, bullying, and shunning those who don't fit in. Teens can be really horrible people, too. These actions are probably your worst fault, but I wonder where you learned them?

School says yes to the rah-rah of teenage spirit. It likes it because it created it. Without school, there would be no cheerleaders and no football stars, no geeks and nerds, no popular kids and no outcasts. Just wait until you hit university, if you go. All of the garbage of high school is radically stripped away overnight. No one cares who you were or what you did in high school. If you bring it up, it will be seen as immature. Grade twelve, your senior year, that's it. After prom night and graduation, you're on your own, and none of your accomplishments will mean anything.

There's yet another secret we have been lying to you about—the idea that what you are now is what you will always be, that school is the be-all and end-all of life. If you are a loser in school, academically or socially, then for your entire life you will be one of the biggest losers. If you really believe in this, it can cause disasters.

Like Columbine. The two fellows who shot up the place were tragic and ironic believers in the junk that they claimed to abhor. They had no perspective because schooling gives none. They thought that their lives were set in stone, and that what happened to them in school was what their whole life was about. They wandered the rooms and hallways picking specific kids to kill. They planned the bloodbath and carried it out. No rational human being would ever do anything close to this. But rationality requires experience and perspective, the very two things that schooling seeks to avoid teaching you. Some say that school shootings are about kids who have been bullied. This is only a little part of the story.

The biggest lie that some schools, some teachers, and some administrators tell you is that school should be the most important thing in your life. No. It is one of the least important. Why?

Aside from being a warehouse—call it a daycare if you want to speak of elementary schools—its main goal is social control and conformity. It gets you while you're young and makes you into what it wants. This does not sound like a good idea for you. In fact, adults spend a lot of their lives getting over what school has done to them. (We will see later that we also need to do this with family as well, to really become who we are meant to be.)

University can help. Ironically, while the college system looks very much like a larger high school, all the social problems of high school are gone. The university system presents to you its own kind of problems, like lying about the relevance of what it teaches or idealizing its role in society. But at least it does not foster cliques, reward popularity, or force you to be like the prettiest or handsomest goody-two-shoes kid in the place. This is because you are suddenly adults. The university might not treat you exactly like full adults, but legally it does not need to look after you. Universities are essentially bureaucracies, and although certain employees may care about young people, the institution as a whole has no legally binding obligation to you.

This is a good thing. Because the responsibility that adults in specific social roles like teaching feel toward you is laced with a strong desire to control you. You must conform, or society will fall apart. Not true. Society might change, but it won't fall apart. The history of schooling reads like the history of prisons. Indeed, they are very similar institutions, along with nursing homes, asylums, and the military. Students of society call them 'total institutions.' This means that you come in being one thing and come out the other end being completely different.

Try this simple experiment: Can you recall anything about yourself as a person before you entered kindergarten? If you are fifteen to nineteen or so now, what were you like at four? And where did that person go? Schools don't make people. They *replace* them. They remake them. Think of your substitute teachers. Yeah, you can slack off and treat them like garbage—way to go! Nice people, teenagers, right? But think about this: Schools love your *substitute persons*. You have gone along with school and killed off your younger selves. No more four-year-old. Later on, no more twelve-year-old. Insofar as these are necessary steps to growing up, one needs to do it. But think of the sacrifice. Where did all your childhood imagination go? It is not entirely fair to say that television sucks people's minds out, as popular music songs have often stated. Maybe it does. But people have to be taught to watch TV, too. The conformity and passivity necessary for teenagers to sit in front of TV for hours on end comes from schooling. What do you think you do in school?

But the greatest sacrifice schooling wants you to engage in is perspective. While a teen does not want to solely rely on the judgment of a little kid, the cumulative memory of what you have been is in fact what you are now. We are not radically different persons during our life. We are not the same persons we were, for sure. But there is a continuity of our persona. We can't just turn personality traits off and move on. We need the perspective of whom and what we have been. Ironically, it is in retirement when adults often recover activities they had started as a child, like certain hobbies. Wow. Kill your child self off, then bring him or her back to life just before you die. Sounds like a great idea! No wonder games and movies about zombies are so popular these days. We are not scared of the dead coming back to haunt us. *We are scared that we might already be dead, and this fear is what is haunting us.* School is the biggest assassin of children in the modern world.

Here's another story. I knew this person growing up who in school was quite marginal. His grades were mediocre. He was part of the nerdy, dateless group. This person did not seem to have much of a future. Two years into university, nothing much had changed. But in third year, something happened. He found something that was obviously very interesting. Suddenly his grades skyrocketed. He won major academic awards. He went on to graduate school. Now he holds not one but two PhDs and is a high-level administrator at a small college. He married and has what we call a normal life. Isolation, nerdiness, marginality, apparent slowness of mind—all vanished without a trace. *This* is an example of the perspective that I am saying is almost completely lacking in schools. What you are *now* is exactly that—just now. Not your life. Not some other time. Not history.

Being a teenager in school is for some of you going to be the worst time in your life. Another big lie is teachers and parents and others telling you over and over again that this is the best time in your life. Hardly. You already know the facts. Who wants to be forced to go to a place every working day and forced to learn things that may have no appeal or relevance? Who wants to be watched outside of school by doing homework and participating in other school-related activities or other activities that the school may not sponsor but are in place to occupy your time? Because God knows, if teens had their own time, things would be a disaster.

Well, of course I have no idea if God knows this. But what I do know is that you are a prisoner of the school system when you are a teenager. And prisoners conform only because they are forced to. We have already seen with drugs and convicts that people 'fake it to make it.' How many of you are just like them?

And it goes farther than this. It *is* true to say that if you drop out your life is going to suck. School makes you into the person who can be viable, who can survive and succeed in the society in which we all live. Without it, you might be marginal economically, socially, and intellectually. School serves the purpose of making an *official* society. Massive countries with hundreds of millions of people cannot ever agree on what a good society is. So schools step in with state-sponsored content and make that decision for us.

You may not know that the origins of schools included a period of great conflict. Most people did not want their kids attending. Not only because it took away their labor force, but more authentically, they knew that it would eventually destroy their culture. What schools did to Native Americans they did to all people, white and non-white. Schooling, from the beginning, sought to make everyone into the same thing. It has succeeded marvelously. It is an institution of a modern and recently developed economic system we call capitalism. It serves capital. It destroys the enemies of capital in a symbolic manner. If you have doubts about what it is turning you into, just look at the adults around you. Do any of them look like revolutionaries to you?

They may complain about the way things are. Do they ever get together and do something about it? Perhaps once in a while, when something comes up that affects them and their children personally. But otherwise, not very much. We've been critical of adults in this book thus far, and there is more to come. But keep in mind throughout that we have enough on our hands just trying to survive for ourselves and our families. We don't have time to start a revolution even if we believed in one. To be fair, regular people don't need revolutions anyway. They need peace of mind, job security, affordable housing, safe workplaces, safe schools for their kids, medical care, and elder care.

I once saw a quip that said, "Revolution is the opiate of the intellectuals." Not bad. Mainly true. For it is the cultural elites that dream up big words and ideas and then think that because everyone must know that they are smarter than everyone else, everyone else should just follow them. More on this in the chapter on politics. Suffice it to say for now that all forms of radical political action entail a reaction that makes most people suffer.

The idea of major and sudden change is a kind of drug. Like all drugs, its use means its abuse. It distracts people from thinking about what they really need, like the practical things in the list above. And this goes for all people around the world. You could add clean air and water, safe food, and safe homes and families too. I am not being conservative when I suggest that meaningful change must be community oriented and come from what people need, not what a few dreamers and artists have imagined.

These ideas should inspire us, perhaps. But they cannot provide the blueprints to a better world. This is another thing school glosses over. Because schooling is about tooling, anything that seems to be too abstract is left out. We graduate from high school or even university without a clue as to what communism was about, for example, or why capitalism seems to be how everyone wants to live today. We come into the world as young adults with a set of vague tools. These tools are then sharpened with job experience or the experience of having a family. There is no time for dreaming in our modern world. We do not need to think to survive.

This is what we are taught. But you cannot be fully human without thinking. The only reason our species even exists is because we outwitted all the others. Though we are having a tough time outwitting ourselves—we are certainly our own greatest enemy, whether at the personal or the species levels—we are unconditionally masters of the world, for better or worse. Even our major religious beliefs hail from the advent of our intellectual and technological abilities to control the world around us. We quite naturally believed that our gods made us into destinies. It is important to note that earlier religions never made such claims. This was so because the people that held them had very little ability to master their surroundings and were in close and ongoing competition with animals and other natural forces. More on this topic later as well. For now, we must recognize that while we have become the stewards of the earth, our stewardship is much in question.

It turns out that we cannot live without thinking, not in the long term. It's like being in love, especially for teens. This is a period of wonder and fulfillment. Everything else goes out the window—school, family, other friends you may have known for years. After a little while, this either settles into a more balanced life or the cherished relationship disappears. You come back to friends, family, and other less important things. As adults, we are a lot more skeptical about love. Indeed, if we become cynical about love we lose the ability to fall in love completely, which is another thing that makes us less than fully human.

But you folks have the ability to love without concern for the implications of being in love. This is a great gift. You can use it in anything you want. It does not have to have anything to do with romance and sex. Your love can be directed to art, science, politics, or what have you. The 'unconcern' of inexperienced loving is not by itself a negative thing. Schooling could benefit from it in a number of ways. For 'unconcern' is, ironically, one of the hallmarks of sincere learning.

Think about most of the learning you do as a teenager. You sit in desks in rows and face the front of the class. An adult talks to you. Not generally *with* you, but to you. You sit there and listen. There may be questions and answers. But we know where the questions and answers are supposed to come from. You question. Adults answer. I did say earlier that you need to be questioning adults all the time. So this is not in itself a bad thing. But the kinds of questions you ask in class are almost all directed to information and clarification. The real 'why' questions that I talked about previously do not get asked. School generally forbids real learning. This is because it is stuffed to the gills with information. Some of it you need to know. Some of it is questionable. Some is utterly irrelevant. You do not get to decide, of course, because we assume that you know nothing worth knowing anyway. Instead of involving teens as a resource in the classroom, teachers strain to control you and keep you on task. They don't even really set the tasks. This is all done at the level of state or other large political region. This is what we refer to as the 'state curricula'. Curricula just mean the stuff you learn in school. Wait a minute! It means more than that. It's the stuff you *have* to learn in school. If you don't, there will be severe penalties. But in fact it's how and how much you have to learn to get where you want to go.

If you really wanted to be a social philosopher and intellectual like me, then you would probably want to get decent grades in courses like history and English. Gym and art might be sidelines, science and math a struggle. But first of all, how many people would ever want to become a philosopher? Second, we have already seen an example of how someone marginal in school became an intellectual with flying colors later on. As a university professor, I see these late bloomers all the time. Whatever their interest, they have one thing in common. They have *fallen in love* with their abilities and their interests. However long this lasts—because, of course, you can fall out of love, too—it provides an unprecedented drive. It allows anyone to thrive at anything they set their mind to. No obstacle is too high. They treat their interest as they would a lover. "Nothing is going to stop me from seeing my girl," I would say to my parents. It was a waste of time and breath, because they had no intention of stopping me.

But you know teens. Some of your very best attributes come out as uncontrolled passions. This said, your humanity is showing itself. Passions lend themselves to the worst excesses humans have ever devised. School *could* help us understand our passions and turn them in the direction of compassion. But what it actually does is stifle and suppress both. Because of the effort needed to really dig deep down into our hearts and minds, school shies away from it. Because of the care and concern human beings would need to show each other at all levels, this scene does not fit with schooling and never did. The point of schools was to take young people who used to work in mines, factories, and offices and store them for a while so that they could later on work in mines, factories, and offices. The 'child-saving' movement in the mid-nineteenth century basically created the modern school system. Dangerous work was not for children because they were innocent and could not consent to such conditions. Why are older persons any less innocent of the dangers of work? Why are we able to consent to it? In fact, we generally do not consent to it in any authentic way. Yes, we got 'saved.' We were saved for later use and abuse in the workplace. More on this topic in the following chapter. We need to raise it here because it is school that 'manufactures' our consent to labor. This is the key to understanding what is sometimes called the 'invisible curricula.'

We already know that curricula (plural) is the stuff we are forced to learn. Its invisibility is the reason why we are forced to learn it. It has nothing to do with relevance. That is why most teens question it in that way. Teenagers in particular are suspicious that something else is going on around them. But you can't see it. Because it is invisible, something other than our usual way of thinking must be applied to it. It must be exposed. When a pretty girl says to her math teacher, "When am I ever going to need to know math in my modeling career?" we could respond with, "Well, you might want to know if your agent and accountant are cheating you out of your millions." This entails a basic knowledge of math that in fact we all need to have. Not trigonometry.

But even the basics are used by the schools as a decoy. They distract us from the more pressing and deeper questions. Because we truly *do* need to know the basics in every discipline, we attend to them. They are an ally of the other stuff that we may not need to know depending on what we think we want to do with our lives. Of course, you have also heard adults tell you that as a teenager you cannot really know what you want to do. This is a horribly mixed message. One the one hand, we tell you that this is all you will ever be. On the other hand, we tell you that you don't even know what you could be. Great stuff. Hard to know what to do with that. What teens tend to do with it is think that their potential future interests will just come to them because of who they already are. You as a person are already complete. You just need to add some interests and make some money. Want fries with that?

The secret here is that you are of course far from complete. And in fact the future interests you may or may not develop add to your person. They are not an overlay. You are not a car with your undercoat waiting for the paint job that will turn people's heads. But this is sure how school treats you. School seeks to turn out a million unpainted cars. Your later experiences, jobs, family life, and health will provide the finishing touches. We can spend our retirements polishing our fenders. Nothing else is needed. This is the biggest 'lie my teachers told me.' Of all the calculated errors of official political history, the lies about our own current history are the worst and most dangerous, namely textbooks that are dishonest about what actually occurred or that censor voices out the past.

These lies come in a package. They create alliances with the stuff you *are* actually taught in school. It does not matter if that stuff is correct or not. In math, for instance, it must always be correct. In science, mostly so. Scientific topics like evolution are played down in some regions, for example. In some Catholic schools that I know of, scientific discovery is explained as humanity understanding God's vision through nature. Perhaps this is true. But the two systems don't generally get along with each other.

In English, the stuff is correct insofar as it represents a certain style and tradition of communication. If you speak Ebonics, 'standard' English will seem biased and very 'white.' But it is in history class that the lies are most focused. And there is every reason for this to be the case. Math you can take anywhere. Same with science. Everyone in the world seems to be learning some version of English because it is the language of commerce and trade. It also has come to the fore because it was the language of a global empire that lasted for three hundred years. Great Britain made sure that people in Nigeria, India, South Africa, and a host of other nations leaned English, whatever else they might learn. The elites of the same countries today still send their kids to England to be schooled. It is one of the finest marks of status money can buy. Even Harvard is not seen as quite as good in these circles. And this is just a minor example of why history is the subject that is taught in the most dishonest way.

First of all, high school history is notoriously boring. This boredom is created on purpose. Teens might want to know more about history if it were taught in another way. But a series of disconnected dates and events, and a focus on warfare, nation-building, competition among nations, alliances, battles, and the odd hero overcome any interest you guys might feel to look deeper. You are taught a certain version of why this or that war started. But do you get asked to think about the question, "Why war?"

All of the assumptions of the nation-state are brought into play in history class. *This* is the way *we* live. *This* is the way *you* are going to live. No questions arise about our economic system. No questions are posed about our giant militaries. No questions are asked about job and status hierarchy. No questions address the class system. We have come far to begin to ask questions about race and gender. But notice how these questions are always directed to the rights of non-whites and females to get in on the action. Almost never do you hear voices that question the system as it is. No. We are okay with previously marginalized people joining us, as long as they are going to support what is as is. No real changes allowed. Once in a while the music you listen to asks some other kinds of questions. But who is listening? Or is pop culture just another decoy that turns us into dreamers rather than doers?

We have already seen, and will talk again later, about how radical action is likely to end in disaster. Even so, we need to be thinking and working toward a better society for all. We cannot simply say to ourselves, "Ah, I am finally invited to the table and can take my piece of the pie." Media stories about women in the boardroom, minority medical researchers and scientists, women and minority politicians. Yawn. All this does is reinforce the idea that the way in which we are living now is not only the best way, but the only way.

We do not even ask about all those people who have voted with their feet, who want nothing to do with our status and money-hungry system of labor and schooling. We don't see them because they have already taken themselves out of the game. And the numbers who are doing so are increasing each year.

If you're a true teenage cynic, you might say, "Good for them. Bunch of losers. It just means more for me." This attitude might take you far in our world. I wonder how many friends you'll have. I wonder if the person who marries you isn't all about using you. A religious-oriented person would question your morals. And in the end, you can't take it with you, wherever you are going. You could of course say, "Who cares" to all of this as well. But I am betting most of you won't. Teens are not by nature nasty, selfish brats, and all of us, adults as well, can easily fall into acting like we are. The entire system of schooling, and later on, work, celebrates it. We may not like the people who do it most successfully. But we sure do envy the fruits of their success: money, power, fame, the ability to do whatever they want. It all starts with the schools.

Teachers are trained to reward not only conformity but those who are 'keeners,' teenagers who have not only learned to conform but also ask only 'appropriate' questions. For those of you who seem to relish this behavior, school loves you the most. You're the least problematic. Think of the homes and families you tend to come from. Mostly, all is calm. You're not afraid of your parents. Sometimes you don't even see them that often. You're almost certainly middle class or higher. You assume university and a professional job is in your future. Why you? Are you so much better a person than your peers? No. You have the opportunities laid out for you. We already know that no one asks to be born. You got lucky. The person sitting beside you didn't. It makes all the difference in the world.

Cynicism is only the nastiest response to this reality. Pity is a bit better. Compassion and concern are much better.

Changing the system from within is better still. But stop there, because if we step outside of the system and attempt to alter it in some grandiose manner, the whole thing will fall in on us. That is only part of what we wanted—we are now under the rubble, after all—and how do you rebuild from the chaos of rubble?

Recognize schools for what they are and what they do. Maintain your distance from them. You have to go to them to get out of them. "If you're going through hell, keep going," as someone cleverly suggested. You need schools more than they need you. This is a huge problem, but you can turn it to your advantage. I often say to my first-year students that if they were really serious about not liking exams and having to pay tuition that they should simply not show up. All of them. All at once. I guarantee there would be changes that they want worked out. It might take some time. Not everyone will agree on everything. But this is how it begins: organization and action, small steps with a larger vision, nonviolent, and respectful. We do not (yet) live in a dictatorship. There is no need to take to the streets in some uncontrolled and threatening way. More on this later.

Here's an example: You find history boring. You tell us how to teach it. You tell us what you want to know about. What you *need* to know about, now, in your lives. You might want to know *why things are the way they are*. What teenager doesn't? Oh yeah, the ones out of touch with drugs, video-games, obsessed with sports or appearance, worried about being abused at home, or having enough to eat, or about being 'invited' into a gang. Sound like some of you? All the more reason to make school into the place where you can really find out the things you need to know, not what adults say you need to, at least not always. After all, I'm an adult, and I'm telling you what I think. I may be wrong. But if I am, you can find that out too. The difference between learning one version of history by rote and coming to understand how and why people lived and acted one way rather than another is the difference between history and what we can call 'historical consciousness.' It's simple enough. You want to become conscious, alert, focused, knowledgeable, and interested about history. History is quite literally what we are. The old line about forgetting history and then repeating it is certainly part of this argument. But the person who said that one wasn't stupid. He also went right on to say that even if we recall history, we might still repeat it. So it really does matter the *way* in which we remember. This goes for anything.

If we were abused and later said that it was okay for adults to do that to us, or that we 'deserved' it, then we feel a certain way about ourselves. Same goes for whole countries and peoples. Historical consciousness does not stop asking questions of itself. It does not make you into a neurotic, anxious person to investigate just what it was that lead to your actions, the actions of others, or the events that are now understood to be historical. Why this history? What about all the other histories out there? Why do Iranians think differently from us? What about the Chinese? Surely *that* many people couldn't just be making junk up. And how the heck did people like the Taliban ever get started, much less get real power for a while?

This is just a tiny sample of questions that, as an emerging adult, you need to think about. This is our world *as it is*. Not some imaginary fable. Not the world of our dreams and ideals. Not the world in which we live and all others are just here. Teenagers are always surprised by the end of high school. As I mentioned before, after graduation no one cares what you did, who you did, and where you are going, if anywhere. Only you care. The world is all of a sudden a very lonely place. If you know how the world actually works and why, you will at least be prepared to step into it with some confidence. With caution and alertness, yes, but not fear, not loathing, and perhaps more to the point with teens, without arrogance, as if you're the best thing since Edison.

I have never gone to a high school reunion. There have been several by now. My junior and senior years, grade eleven and twelve, were the two worst years of my life, and not because I understood what was going on. Quite the opposite. I still won major awards, had enough friends, played a lot of music, and participated in class. I was a nuisance to teachers because I was apparently smart enough to be skeptical but not smart enough to know what to do with my skepticism.

I had very little fun. I was not happy in any sense of the word. School exacerbated what was going on in my home life. It was not a refuge. It added anxieties. It made friends into competitors. It made skeptics into enemies. I only found out the obvious truth long after. I was not alone. When I ask my own students—thousands, over the years—what's the greatest thing about university, they say simply, "It's not high school."

We know the university sucks in its own way, too. But on this point they are correct. And you can do a lot with that simple knowledge. Aside from coming into your own as an intellect, like the person I mentioned earlier, you can choose a vocation, not only a work life, but something you might actually be interested in. What a joy to be paid for liking what you do. Huge bonus there. You hear this with people in the elites of certain sports, like golf. They always say when asked about the greatest thing about their work life: "I'm blessed to be able to do what I love to do for a living." Golf might not be the best example. It's so competitive that even the very best might not get paid week in week out, depending on their performance. There are no salaries in competitive golf. But it serves the purpose of suggesting that you can use school as a way to know the kind of person you do *not* want to be. Most of the things school favors turn people against one another. People compete for grades, university entrance, program entrance, and then jobs. At the same time, if you maintain your distance and find yourself in the top shelves, you suddenly have a chance to make the world better. There is a sacrifice to be made with schooling. It's a big challenge to make it worth your while. Do the work you need to do to get to where you have a chance to make your own decisions. Don't ever believe that school is the last stop, or that how you are defined in school has anything to do with who you really are. We all know about labeling kids. The 'bad' kids are forever bad; the 'good' can do no wrong.

In our society school is going to be with us for a long time—maybe not parts of the university, but certainly the lower levels. We can't do without it. As adults, we use it in a number of ways. It keeps our teens off the streets and from burning down our houses. It allows us to slack off on 'discipline' and the real work of helping you to become an adult. It saves us from learning all the stuff you have to learn. Like I said earlier, I doubt I could pass a grade-twelve math course at the moment. It shifts the responsibility away from families. It takes teens out of the private and into the public. It allows adults to be more private and less public. School makes adults annoyed when the state curricula contradicts our customary or personal beliefs, but in general, trust me, adults *love* school. How could we not. We're not in it! So don't come to us for help on this one. We're definitely the enemy.

Insofar as school provides necessary basic skills in certain subject areas, insofar as it provides the space where one learns to coexist in a wider community of peers and instills certain habits that you need to use later in life for survival, school can't be all bad. But since school's main purpose is to store and change kids from curious, enchanted new human beings full of wonder to passive producers and consumers full of anxiety and false needs, I am going to rate school a three out of ten.

5. The Secrets of Work (and money)

〰〰〰〰〰〰〰〰〰〰〰〰〰〰〰〰〰〰〰〰〰〰〰〰〰

"And if you think school is tough, try working for a living." How many times have adults thrown this old line out at you? This time, however, there is some truth to it. And it's this truth that I would like to talk with you about in this chapter.

We have come to see 'work' and 'labor' as the same thing. Before the full impact of the industrial revolution was felt throughout society, there was a crucial distinction between the two words. Labor was something you did to survive. Peasants labored in the fields. Smiths labored in the forge. But work was reserved for the privileged few. 'Work' meant more of what we would think of today as a 'life's work.' My work then would not have anything directly to do with mere subsistence. Rather, it would define my existence. It would even include objects I would use to do my work. Think of the famous Olympic cyclist without her bike, or the awesome rock guitarist without his axe. When we see these people in the media they almost always have the tools of their higher trade with them. Otherwise we might see them as just another person, like us. So while today we almost always see work as a negative thing—I have to go to work. I have to get some work done. Thank God it's Friday—we still are able to dimly recognize that a few of us have found something that not only puts food on the table but somehow defines us as human beings.

It is this ability to define ourselves by our work that has been generally lost in modern society. Instead, we labor. And in our economic system we mainly labor for other people, not ourselves. We work for the government through taxation.

We work for owners of business through the profits they make from our labor. At first glance this seems to make no sense. Even in school you get the grade you apparently deserve. There is at least an official or ideal relation between your labor and your reward. Not so with work. Taxes are necessary to pay for services we could not pay for as individuals. Many countries disagree on the thresholds here. In the United States, there is more onus on the individual to pay his or her way. In Canada, it's more the government's responsibility. In Europe, even more so. Same with what services are public and private. When I lived in the USA, I always did a double take when I saw the liquor shelf in grocery and box stores. In Canada, in most regions, the sale of certain kinds of substances is much more tightly controlled. It's a bit of a shell game, though. In the USA you can buy some booze and walk down the aisle and pick up some bullets too. This might not seem like a good combination, but most people do not associate them in this way. But in Canada, where you would get the smug smirk of 'that's why we're better than you' going on, you can do exactly the same thing. You just might have to go to different stores. Big deal.

So both work and its fruits are controlled in slightly different ways depending on where you live. There are age restrictions on both production and consumption, as teenagers well know. Once again, it's all about adults deciding when it's time for you to be like us. It might be a challenge to do this on an individual basis, but it would be fairer. But one thing you are expected to do in becoming an adult, no matter who you are and where you come from, is work. Or rather, *labor*, because work is now a lucky strike for the very few. These people have figured out how to earn enough money for their needs and wants while at the same time loving how they earn. And not because their work earns. It is precisely because the earning part of labor is no longer an issue for them that they have turned it into their *work*. They have made labor into work. In today's way of doing things this is apparently rare and difficult. Yet this is the only society in history where most people can even think about doing that. In ancient and medieval times, work was for the very few. Slaves and peasants did the dirty labor of keeping society going. A few elite persons, almost always men of the highest caste or class, could work as philosophers and religious thinkers—many were the same thing in those times—or political figures and royalty. Even artists, who today often try to exempt themselves from the labor cycle, were not considered to be doing 'work', but they were considered to be highly skilled and therefore more expensive laborers.

It is interesting that new religions that preached equality, like Christianity, first spread through the ancient world through the artisan classes. It is likely this occurred because those people were in constant contact with elites, serving them. They were made aware that in their own minds at least, they were much more talented than their masters. This alone would put them in the mood to try on a religion that offered a higher judgment than that of humankind. God knew the truth of things and would set things right.

Slaves, on the other hand, were not only thought of as subhuman, they internalized this definition over thousands of years. They rarely encountered their real masters and did not imagine themselves as talented. Christianity therefore cannot be referred to as a 'slave religion' in any literal or historical sense. As long as social organization was built on forced labor, the amount of room for authentic work to appear was small and open only to the elite.

Today, however, we are still forced to labor. We now work for a salary, hence the odd sounding but strangely apt phrase 'wage-slavery,' which ironically opens up the space of work. We see famous 'workers' regularly, pop stars and athletes, for instance, even though we recognize them as elite. But not all people who have found their vocation are famous. I use this word in an old-fashioned sense as well. It originally meant your calling, as from God. You're on this earth to do this and this alone. It is your life and it is God's purpose that you fulfill it in this specific way. A few people still believe in this. It's not a bad way to look at things, especially if you really want to do something and there are bumps in the road.

People with a sense of vocation are often able to overcome obstacles in their path. They feel that this is their calling, whether from God or not, and they work very hard to attain their goals. Most of the time other people benefit from their work. Work tends to create community, unlike labor. Of course, we know dictators who have claimed a calling too.

'Wage-slavery' may be a little extreme. But all of us are required to labor, and most of us around the world labor for very little. When people labor for bare survival and sometimes not even enough for that, it does call to mind the older slavery. The key to slavery is that you are not *free*. Modern labor usually does not free us, or only at long last when we retire. Of course, unlike the old slaves, we can walk away. But to what? When there is a poor decade in terms of the economy, we know what happens. Your parents lose their jobs. They have to move or go on welfare, perhaps. Your quality of life plummets. Your friends change. You go to a new school in a worse part of town with people you don't know, and what's more, with people you thought you'd never know.

All of this is very scary. But we need to remind ourselves that most people around the world are already there. Downward social mobility is a sign of recent times in North America. There are a few regions, like where I live, where it's the opposite. But over the past decade, things have been tough almost all over. Some companies take advantage of that by hiring at lower wages. With more laborers out of a job, there are fewer jobs and lower pay. It's a dreary but almost inevitable equation. Some economists thought it was a natural principle. But clearly it is our fellow humans who are manipulating the strings. The puppet laborers, the rest of us, better perform or the strings will be suddenly cut.

The point is not to avoid working for a living. The ideal would be to copy what a few have attained. Not all of us can be popular, let alone famous through our talents. But most of us, perhaps all of us, given the right series of opportunities can be happy in our jobs and feel like we are making a serious contribution to society. For we owe a living not only to ourselves but to our communities. Work-sharing might be a good idea for highly paid professionals who work long hours. You see these people all the time. Perhaps your parents are some of them. In business, health, law, and politics especially, these wealthy persons drive the luxury vehicles and live in the large homes, but they also work sixty to eighty hours per week.

True confession: that's the biggest reason why I've stuck around as a professor—short hours and good pay. Students come and go. You can have a brief, good influence on a young person's life, but it sure doesn't replace family. And with almost all jobs, there are always people who don't want you around. So you have to cut your losses and weigh the options. Do I love this enough to stick to it? How do the positives and negatives balance? Does it take me away from things in life that are more important? Some of you hardly ever see your parents. You grew up with the net, video games, and TV as your babysitters. Perhaps because of absent parents young people sometimes crowd around professors, hoping to get some adult advice and even TLC.. These brand new adults—slightly older versions of you—have not had any adult role models close at hand. Suddenly *they* are the adults, and they don't know what they're doing.

Well, God help them, I sometimes think, looking back at the troubles I have had in my life. What a great role model to choose! The girls are charming, of course. The guys, affable. The presence of the females always makes my wife laugh. Obviously I maintain my distance. It's a bit of a joke. Being a professor suggests to people two things: you're supposedly smart, and you're probably arrogant. A minor secret: professors are trained to be researchers and not teachers. If you do get a good teacher in university, it's simply a lucky coincidence. Don't graduate from high school and then expect the university to save you. It can't, not at an individual level or at an institutional level. To be fair, the stuff we teach—philosophy, history, sociology, psychology—might have the power to get you where you want to go. Latch on to the 'discourse' and *not* to professors. The commonplace view of professors is often true. We are clever in our own way, but we really like to flaunt it.

But back to work. What I just said was relevant because a lot of people look to their workplaces to save them from other parts of their lives that may not be going well. We all know workaholics. These people live to work. We should only be working, or laboring, to live, and not the opposite. Even teens can get this way. Straight A's don't come easy for most. But numerous people can pull it off. I always wonder a little when I see students who are consumed with schoolwork. I wonder if there is something that they are running from. In an odd way, the honor roll students and the dropouts might share more than they think. Some of both may be escaping a harsher reality. Once in a while you hear of teens who are threatened with punishment if they don't make the grade. But this I think is rare. You can't get good results through threats, either in school or at work. Employers and their psychologists who consult for them have long ago decided that rewards work far better than punishments. Well, what kinds of rewards are out there for us?

For teens, earning money or having it means you can spend it, almost always on stuff you want. Some of you might be in need of food or other necessities, however, so money takes on a new meaning. For adults, spending money takes two forms: paying off the regular debts of living and buying something for pleasure. It is difficult to set a boundary between the two. This is because in our society *wants have become needs*. Just as we now no longer usually make the distinction between work and labor, we also have muddled wants and needs. So some of us 'need' larger houses, faster or larger vehicles, and vacations more exotic than the last. Most of us 'need' variety in our eating, or 'need' to go out to a restaurant twice a week. We sneer at you because you don't really need anything. Your basic needs are supposed to be satisfied by us adults. But we are actually worse at making the distinction than you are. North America has about five percent of the world's population. We use fifty percent of the world's energy and generate about seventy-five percent of the world's waste. No surprise. We live high on the hog here and have done so for almost a century. This lifestyle comes at the expense of others. But these others are almost always out of sight and out of mind. This situation bothers us to a point. We are not totally ignorant of it. But its full implications are so hard to stomach that we suppress it.

I once saw a graffito in my hometown of Victoria, Canada. Victoria is a wealthy city in a beautiful setting. Tourists flock there year-round, most of them from the USA. The message spray-painted on the concrete was, "Third World Blood fuels your lifestyle." Short and to the point. Rather graphic and disturbing because there is truth in it. Not long after it appeared, someone else, obviously unhappy with the original sentiment, spray-painted 'CRAP' over it.

Well, no single statement can encapsulate a complex situation. But the combination of the two was insightful. We *do* live in our way at the expense of others, sometimes to their injury and death. To an extent, our pleasure is the other's suffering. But it is also true that we are not only aware of this, we don't like it, so much so that the graffiti critic needed to quickly try to nullify the original message. Would just this simple four-letter word reassure us that we are good people at heart?

Teens might be suspicious of this global situation. Your energies get turned to charity and volunteer work, which is not a bad thing in principle. But it's a Band-Aid. It does not address the roots of the problem. The key to this odd situation is the relationship between overproduction and overconsumption. The other thing people do not think about when they are critical of global geopolitics and our collective role in it is that we in wealthy countries are not happy about the way we have to work either. Most people are overworked. Most rewards are fleeting. Work erodes community and family. We also obsess over work in ways others do not.

Yet it is also true to say that increasingly around the world people very different from us are getting into the idea that work is their savior. It is bitterly ironic that a similar message, this time in ironwork, hung over the gates of the biggest death camp in World War Two. At Auschwitz, the message to the arriving victims was, "Work sets you free."

There it meant that if you worked hard you would die more quickly. In our own smaller and much less forced way, there are many of us who have taken this dictum to heart as well. We already mentioned workaholics. These people sacrifice their health, relationships, longevity, and quality of life to the work god. Or, if not exactly to labor itself, then to the god which the whole world seems to be getting around to worshipping, the god of money.

Labor as work can be addicting. The biggest thing that fuels this addiction is money. More money means more power to do the things you want. But time slips away. The money piles up. Your health fades and your ability to do these once-dreamed of things fades as well. The work/labor/money addiction is just as bad as any drug. It destroys just as many human ties. It makes you think you live in your own world. More money means you can manipulate the world the way you want, reinforcing this fantasy. But the world is not our own. No person is an island entire of itself. We dream of being free. But what kind of freedom is involved here? Who pays for our freedom?

I mentioned two technical terms above: 'overproduction' and 'overconsumption.' What do they mean for us? For a long time, industrial production—factories, mills, railroads, and the like—produced much less than society actually needed. It took about 150 years, from the start of the industrial revolution in England, to fill up the needs of an ever-growing society and global network of nations. Then, around 1925, for the first time in human history, we reached a point where technologies in factories caught up. We could now produce more than we actually needed. There was instantly a surplus of stuff, which people would not buy. If they did, they would simply be duplicating what they already had. Even wearing stuff out, like clothes and tractors, did not happen fast enough to reduce the surplus. Something had to be done.

One might think we would have simply tried to sell the stuff to people around the world. But these people had no use for it and could not purchase it to make that kind of sale worthwhile. And we were not just going to give it away, though that might also seem to be the right thing to do.

What actually happened was the birth of modern advertising. In the very same year as overproduction was attained, the first book on how to sell items people did not need appeared. It was written by a professor of psychology. In fact, this guy was the founder of what came to be called 'behaviorism.' This meant simply that some people thought others could be molded into whatever they wanted by repeating tasks and demands and issuing punishments and rewards to them. It became extremely influential in the twentieth century. We still try to make you folks into adults by using some of the same techniques. Teach, observe, repeat. It is one of the reasons why school and work are often so boring. Most jobs are in fact behaviorist, repetitive tasks. We keep things simple, with no thinking necessary. Sometimes, depending on where you end up working, it's "no thinking allowed." We pay 'better' people than you to do the thinking for you. And what happened in 1925 was that very thing. A professor who thought he knew how the human mind worked simply said, "If you want to sell junk people don't need, you've got to convince them to buy it." You do that by making them think that if they buy your product, they will be better people. In other words, *the more and better stuff you have, the better you.* "The person who dies with the most toys wins," as a bumper sticker says. (I also have seen bumper stickers that say, "The person who dies with the most toys still dies," but this more correct sentiment seems to be lost on us.)

In order to make us believe that if we buy this or that we will feel or even be better, advertising had to change. If you look at old ads from before the mid-1920s—say a Sears-Roebuck catalogue—you immediately notice that something is missing. All you get is a description of the item, its price, what it does, and maybe a hand-drawn picture. Nothing else. No hot girls laying on hoods of cars or sipping beer. No stunning landscapes where the Lone Ranger sits on his mount smoking. No sights and sounds at all, in fact. Just the facts: What is it? What does it do? How much is it? Sometimes, as delivery times were sketchy in those days, you'd get an estimate of when it might arrive at your door. But no promises, no guarantees. This was advertising from about the mid-nineteenth century to the mid-1920s. Pretty boring stuff. Not at all the kind of thing that makes you want to go out and buy anything at all unless you really needed it.

But that is the whole point. Production during those days could supply our needs, after a fashion, and nothing else. But nothing else was really present. The 'something else' that had to be created was done so in a very artificial and manipulative way. This is the biggest secret about modern consumption. It's recent and it's unnecessary. It was invented more or less by a single person who thought he knew the human soul. Is our soul really limited to desire for status and lust for wealth? Maybe it is now, after almost a century of modern advertising, but surely it was not always so. However that may be, we are certainly stuck with overconsumption, and that means being stuck with overproduction too. The ads worked like a charm. They continue to do so.

Advertising has had to change to follow changes in society. Sometimes too, ads could change the very society they were marketed in, like the first ads selling overproduced items did. Case in point: In between the World Wars, as many women as men drove vehicles of all kinds. The car was just another tool and was not 'gendered' in the sense that we are more used to. The idea that men drove and women rode is from the post-war period. But more on that in a second. So in the 1920s and 1930s, car ads had just as many handsome young men leaning on the cars as they did pretty women. The selling point was doubled; if you had a car like the one in the picture, you would be seen as this hot guy or girl, but also, you'd be able to pick up the hot guy or girl as well. This would no doubt make you a better person. In your own eyes, this would happen because you were approaching a commercial ideal of beauty and material attainment. But more importantly, you'd be seen as a better person in the eyes of another. And not just any other—another that you wanted to be with and be like. And this other person now wants to be with you and be like you, whereas before she or he did not. Why? Because *before* you were just another dork without this car, or these clothes, or whatever.

Car ads changed radically after the end of the Second World War. This was in response to a wider trend that we are still trying to recover from today. Your grandparents worked through a tremendous world crisis, the scale and horror of which had never before been seen. In order to do so, women went to work in the factories. They tested fighter planes. They tested artillery and small arms. They trained for battle. They were spies. They worked in combat zones as nurses and doctors. This is the Rosie the Riveter story. *Women* did all these things for the first time. And you know what? *They liked it.* All the cool stuff men got to do was opened to women with the exception of actual combat. Not that going to war and killing each other is a wonderful thing for men. But when the war ended, this critical experiment ended as well. Women were pissed at this. There were demonstrations at factories and marches and calls for equality in the workplace. Men had to have 'their' jobs back. "Hey, thanks for the help, girls, but you can go home. The war's over. We don't need you anymore, and you should have never had to this men's work anyway." But this history is often forgotten, covered over by a new, official history that we can call the "gender resocialization project."

This sounds very technical, but all it means is that governments and industry worked together to reinstall the 'feminine' back into women. No problem with the guys. If anything, they needed to calm down after killing and dying for their respective countries. They were *too* masculine after the war. But so were women. Or so it was thought. So this is where you get all the cheesy, hokey ads from TV and magazines showing women the way they were supposed to behave—at home, first and foremost, a mother, yes, but more so, a *housewife*. This is when this term, so derided today, took off. And it was not even looking after the kids that took center stage.

The key to the 1950s' dream was that the home *itself* was to be perfect. The kids could go out and play all day or be at school. They were not the mom's chief duty. No, a woman needed to be a wife first, mom second. And a wife looked after the home, yes, but also her man. Even jokes that suggested, "Greet your husband at the door wearing nothing but a smile," were not too far from the truth. Not that I wouldn't like my wife to do that! But you can see where the project is going. The global crisis had upset gender boundaries and norms, it was said. We needed to get them back on track. But in fact, before World War Two, gender boundaries were not at all what they were to become afterward. The Depression had already seen to that. As we said, the 1920s was a time of unprecedented liberty for women: driving, working out of the house, marrying late, having fewer children. So the idea for the new advertising was to sell much more than objects; it was to sell *what people were supposed to be*.

That a lot of the content of this new kind of person, both woman and man, came from Nazi home propaganda didn't seem to bother anyone either. The Nazis were very '1950s' in the 1930s. If you look at their films on what a proper home and marriage should be like for the emerging super race, they were basically the same stuff that North Americans and others were fed in the fifties. Mothers and daughters should always be dressed as if life were an ongoing party. The party dress had its vogue then, with lots of frills and petticoats. The Walt Disney girl as the ideal young woman appeared at this time, as did the cheerleader and the football star. This was not only how society was supposed to be, it was akin to what nature, or God, had intended for us. The irony of all of this was that it didn't actually work on those it was targeted at.

Your grandparents had been through something that had altered them for good. No one could have survived the Depression and war on that scale and not be changed, usually for the worse. The whole world was in fact a more modest and less intense version of the concentration camp. Anxiety was constant. Fear about the future was in your face, and not just a vague thought once in a while as it might be today. No one knew how things were going to turn out. For many, each day might be their last. For others, those they knew and loved might be never seen again. Teenagers lied about their age to sign up. My dad did just that. In Germany and Russia, most people your age were killed. This is what global war does.

So no sentimental journey back to the nonexistent days of frills and aftershave was going to fix these wounds. But what the gender-resocialization project *did* accomplish was it made these people's kids into perfect little misses and young men. *And these kids became your parents.* Advertising, propaganda, schooling, the obsession over school sports, the desire to be beautiful, the drive to get married and have children, all of this the youngsters sucked in. Their jaded parents pretended to do so, to a point. But they never could leave behind the knowledge of their terrible experiences. They perhaps unwittingly contributed to your parents' focus on highly gendered roles and norms by thinking they needed to protect their children from horror. At the same time, when these kids, your parents, did have problems, *their* parents told them to shut up. This was also a time when children were physically punished on a routine basis. The 1950s was the era of spanking and worse. Why so? Simply because your grandparents had lost something in the crisis: their per-spective on what was a problem or not. Since everything that happened to them was huge, the stuff their kids had prob-lems with they considered to be nothing at all. So they ig-nored it. Finally, your parents' generation rebelled and we had the 1960s and 1970s. But this rebellion was itself made into a commodity, stuff you could buy and consume. The period of real revolution was over. The *project* had done its work.

So what you're left with today is a memory of how guys and girls are supposed to act. Indeed, I am often shocked at how conservative young people are. My students, just slightly older than yourselves, seem to be all about 'being a man' or 'being a woman.' Hey, didn't we leave that behind a long time ago? I wonder. Evidently not. This making sure that you know who you are socially is of course part of be-coming an adult. But being an adult does not have to be any one thing. It seems the work we do to conform exceeds the work we do for money. This is why I have gone on about this topic in this chapter for so long.

The real work we do to make sure we can work and earn money has a lot to do with maintaining expected social roles. Even in areas with full employment, you still notice the drug addict and the person with a mental disability waiting on your table. It's great that they're working, but it underlines what we expect from workers and from ourselves, who also work. To be employable, you must have done all of this work up front. That is why my students are so keen to fit in. Ironic, because from your perspective, you probably can't wait to get out of high school and into university for the reasons we talked about in the previous chapter. But don't be fooled. The older you get, the more you find you have to conform. Partying four nights a week doesn't cut it. It's just another escape from the cold reality of your life: *Be like everyone else, or you're out.*

Out of work, mostly. There's always going to be some other marginal character to have sex or smoke dope with.

But in terms of getting along in the world, let alone being successful, forget it. The world will be much less magical the more you opt out of it.

Another irony is we have turned the meaning of magic inside out. It used to mean something out of the ordinary. Now it can be equated with money. *Money is magic*. Think about it. Magic used to be seen in myth and fantasy as a tool that could get you what you wanted. It could be used for good or evil. Indeed, those who used magic for good became good, if used for evil they became evil. Belief in magic was a way in which societies protected themselves from those who thought they could stand outside society and manipulate it. This was dark magic. This kind of magic upset the order of the universe and of society. The magic of light reset the button. Their conflict was timeless. Each human being had to make a choice as to which side he or she would be on.

This kind of choice is still with us today, though it does not involve trolls, demons, and angels. Those who participate in society are on the side of good. Those who do not are on the side of evil, or at least the bad side. But there is another choice that is involved before you can make the good/bad decision. You have to decide what is actually meant by good and bad. Is it good that people work all their lives for very little money and can only do some things they want to do when they are too old? Is it good that we force you into being like us at an early age without letting you explore yourselves or the world at large? Is it good that we labor for our survival, and if we don't we might starve? Is it good that we have an easy life on the backs of the vast majority of our fellow humans who have a harder life because of it? It is much easier to agree on what is bad: addictions, abuse, violence, dishonesty, much of politics, war, fanatical religion, and militarism. Scientific invention unconcerned with its effects in the world. No problem. Almost anyone can see these as negative. But what of the good?

The stuff I mentioned clearly may be good for some and bad for others. This is the issue. The good is not any one thing. What's good for you might not be good for me. This might even be the case if we both agree that a more abstract quality is good. Education is good. Sure. But education for what? For whom? Health is good. This is a bit easier. But the pursuit of good health can also become an addiction, an obsession, even a major kind of vanity, like iron-pumping.

Would-be athletes aside, most of us know that if we look good we can get a better job. The presentation of yourself means a great deal. For women, it is more work—and there's *that* word again—than for men. But for both sexes it's something you have to concentrate on. More and more I am told what to wear and how to look by advertising. As with all ads, I am aware that if I follow the instructions I will be a better person. *Everything*, not just actual things, can be sold to us, including feelings, looks, smells, likes, and dislikes. Teenagers sometimes scoff at little kids because you are now too old to be fooled by the really stupid ads aimed at your younger siblings. But take a step back and critically review the ads aimed at your age group: the pop bands that industry creates for you; the styles that you must have to be cool. You are being manipulated more than any other age group. This is because you are the people with the most disposable income. You get it from your parents, mostly, and sometimes from part-time jobs. But with no real responsibilities, your income is 100-percent available for consumption. And the ad people know this. They target you like a smart-bomb. You can try to get out of its way, but you'd better run like hell.

But speaking of good and evil, is there anyone we can blame for this ugly situation? Not really, unless we want to blame ourselves for believing the lies that are sold to us. You can't blame the advertisers. They are only trying to make a buck. You can't blame the manufacturers. They are trying to sell their goods. You can't blame governments. They are part and parcel of our economic system. What we *can* do is stop buying stuff we don't need. The system will respond. It will ask us what we want. Then we can tell it that what we want is to avoid the mistakes we are making now: going to work to either just survive or to accumulate needless wealth; laboring longer and longer to get out of needless debt; forcing you folks to conform to the advertised slogans of what makes a good human being; *telling the world to be like us while forcing the world to serve us.* When we change those things, work will have a new meaning and life will open up to us.

I once researched groups of corporate executives. It turns out that they were the same as regular people, except they had more anxiety. They had more responsibility—to their markets, their employees, the environment, and to their businesses. Their mistakes really mattered, and they were very self-conscious about that. Many had developed a sense of mission. They thought they should do more good in the world, though definitions of what was good of course varied widely. They disliked working long hours. They never saw their families. They didn't really enjoy their luxury vehicles that much because they didn't get a chance to really drive them. Their lives sucked in ways that we don't usually think of. They were not evil people. They did not conspire to enslave the rest of us. They had no clue about what they were doing, just like so many others. So before we jump to accuse apparent elites of controlling the world for their own purposes, let's take a look at who is *really* in control.

We are the ones who produce and consume. If we stop doing it the way we do it now, the rest of the problems we associate with overconsumption, like greedy materialism and status competition will follow. We are no longer living in 1925, when a new form of advertising could change the world. Rethinking our work life will be the proof we need to show ourselves to be the more mature society we think we have become.

Work is necessary. It can help build a sense of human solidarity. New and improved sometimes really does mean something. Working does keep some people out of trouble. So we cannot completely dismiss our version of it. But because it enslaves us and makes us passive and unthinking, because it is dull and often meaningless in terms of human fulfillment, and because it is often the source of obsession, I will rate work a three out of ten.

6. The Secrets of Environment (and nature)

~~~~~~

We all live on the same planet. What we do where we live affects others where they live. Maybe these people live on the other side of the earth. It is likely we will never meet them. And the planet itself really is tiny. It is a miniscule speck of dust against the cosmic firmament. It is an insignificant traveler, alone against the vastness of space and time. Its presence, and our presence on it, means nothing to the big picture. The earth has no meaning for anyone or anything that may be out there. It only has meaning for us. We give it its meaningfulness. And it is we who must live with the meanings once they are given.

Human beings are a part of the planet. But we are also apart from it. We are here and not here at the same time. By this I mean that while we live *on* it, we do not live *in* it. Because human beings are not a part of nature in the way all other life as we know it is. Depending on what you believe, this break occurred a very long time ago or quite recently. But it does not matter if God created us with this break or if evolution constructed us with this break. It's the same break. And we can't go back. Nature is forever alien to us, and us to it. If you have ever had an encounter with a wild animal you know this to be true. Nature does not play by our rules. No matter what culture you come from, what your beliefs are, or who you think is a better human being or a worse one, this means nothing to nature. All the jungle books and lion kings and teddy bears mean nothing. Nature plays by its own rules. We are only on the margins of them. We have to respect them to a point. In fact, this chapter is about how we tend to disrespect nature, and the implications affect us all. But nature can also be controlled and altered to a point. How we do that makes all the difference in the world. Quite literally.

We like to think we love nature now. It hasn't always been the case. Nature has often been seen as a challenge, a competitor, or an outright enemy of humans, rather than as a lover. Nature is actually none of these. In the same way nature resists our making it into a part of ourselves through plush toys and animated films, it resists any kind of human relationship. The break between humans and the rest of life was a final one. It may be that we harbor some resentment about that break. We see how animals live. Their lives, however brutal or dull, are much simpler than ours. You can sit on any beach all day, for instance, and even if you are in a city, gradually life will take shape around you. The local wildlife, however small or insignificant, begins to forget you are there. You become part of the scenery if you lie still. Then you can observe how they go about their daily business. It has almost all to do with foraging, or making a living. Animals need to find food. Every day, for most of each day, they do it. From bears to sea hawks, they repeat what to us appears to be the most drab of existences. Of course, once human, we could never go back to only this. Even so, there have been many people who have longed to depart from the complexities of human life.

This longing cannot be satisfied. Hence, a resentment could appear. Why is it so hard just to be human? Why can't we be more like nature? Nature always seems to know what it is doing. Everything in nature has its role. These roles are mostly defined by instincts. That is, when animals and plants come into being, they already know almost everything they need to know to fulfill their destinies. Some large mammals, like lions, for instance, seem to have quite a bit of learned and practiced behavior, such as how to hunt. But most animals, from the tiny specks of bugs to the rhinoceros and hippo, simply set about doing what they do without needing to mull it over in any way. Not so for us. Each decision we make comes with the cost of figuring something out. None of what we do comes naturally. When life appears to be as smooth and poised as a dancer's graceful arc, it is because of long hours of learning and practicing. It is common to say that teenagers are in the life phase of such learning and practicing. From first dates to exams to arts recitals, teens are thrown into new circumstances one after the other. It is bewildering and exciting at the same time. You know more than anyone else at any other life stage what it is to *not* be natural. Your awkwardness is quite literally a sign of your times. Not all adults have mastered even the basics of living as human beings. We have already seen that we are not always the greatest role models for you. This is more evidence that humans do not have instincts. If we did, there would never be any mistakes. No need to learn anything. No need for practice. Adults have to practice too, and once in while we learn something new, generally about ourselves. The fact is that living as a human being is a lifelong learning process. It might come to an abrupt end, but in no way does this exempt us from doing the work in the meantime.

This too might well add to a sense of resentment about nature. An ancient philosopher once said that the biggest difference between humans and nature was that we could not connect the beginning with the end, and never could. Nature *does* make this connection. The plants reappear after a long winter. Spring is like a miracle of rebirth. Animals come out and start their work again. The sun reappears every morning after setting each night. It is the nature of nature to recycle itself. Why then was it left to human beings to be taken out of this cosmic loop of life? This is one of the biggest questions. People have been asking about it for thousands of years. It has to do with finding a purpose. We will talk more about this and related issues in the final chapter. For now, let's just say that because we do find ourselves in this situation, it appears to be up to us to try to give it some meaning.

And that we do. There are so many meanings that if all the teenagers around the world got together, you'd come away thinking that you'll *never* learn how to become an adult! The diversity of human expression is its own miracle. I think it is equal to that of nature's ability to reconnect with itself. For in giving our human lot meaningfulness, we in fact allow ourselves to become human over and over again. New meanings for new people. New lives for old. Children replace the elderly. It's not a perfect and instinctual connection. It may not be cosmic in significance. But it's ours. This is what we can call a paradoxical expression, 'human nature.' The downside of the casual use of that famous phrase is that it becomes an excuse for all kinds of ignorance and cruelty. It is used to justify what are purely historical and social circumstances. You hear adults tell you, "It's just human nature," to get angry, to lust, to want to have children, to abuse power, to seek control, to feel hatred and love, to get revenge, or to be kind. No. None of these has anything to do with nature per se. Nothing about human beings is so natural that it is outside of our capability to change it. All of these basic urges have been altered over the course of history. They do not take the same form in all societies today. Some of them are not even recognizable, like marriage, for instance. Anthropologists have long known that marriage takes as many forms as you can imagine. It might not even be a union with the view to reproduce. Multiple partners of both sexes, same-sex unions, what we would call incestuous partnerships, all are marriage in the world today or historically. The one we are used to, a male and female together taking vows for life, is just one of a great diversity. And yet we tend to think that it is in our nature to seek such a union. Not at all. Never was. So don't just roll over if you think that marriage—or anything else that society tends to want you to do that seems to have nothing directly to do with your health—is maybe not for you, or not yet for you. It takes a great deal of time and effort to become human in all the ways that a culture accepts as being part of the final product. And only as members of a society do we even imagine that there is such a thing. As *individuals*—another idea that is hardly universal and natural—we know differently. We are always unfinished beings, born that way to die that way. Perhaps a God will complete us, but we don't really know for sure.

So between the effort at learning how to live and the fact that there is no one way to do so, we might look at nature with even more longing. In nature, as we said, there is no awkward effort in our sense, no diversity of ways. If you're this animal, then that's it. If you're a plant, then you do what plants do. I wonder if in our longing and resentment, in our historical love-hate relationship with nature, there isn't something that demands of us to either conquer and control it or destroy it, because that is what we are currently doing at an astonishing rate.

By the time you guys are my age, the world might be a difficult place. In fact, a group of scientists and others calling themselves The Club of Rome predicted that by 2042 the environment would reach a tipping point. They first met in 1972 and came up with seventy years for us to alter our ways. We have done a little bit in that direction. Of course, predicting the future is a risky game. But the stakes are far higher than in any other game humans have ever played.

This is so because of who we are, how many of us there are, and how we want to live. Our ancestors lived in tiny numbers compared to us. They occupied a tiny percentage of the earth. The farther you go back, the fewer we were. Large-scale wars started when we developed the technology and grew in population size so that we butted into one another. Before this, we mostly didn't know other people were even alive. Sure, this village up the river sometimes fought with the neighboring village down the river. No big deal. Casualties were light and technologies primitive. No one group could ever get the better of another in any final way. Warfare and the death of cultures in the way we have become used to is a relatively recent thing. It started only about ten thousand years ago with the advent of farming, cities, slavery, record keeping, standing armies, and big government. The people no longer held the power. As well, the religions of many gods started up at this time. The idea that humanity itself had sprung from nothing was fashionable. It's easy to see why if you think of where many of these early civilizations began, by the rare rivers in the great deserts and wastes. The idea that humans were raised from dust and shaped as jars of clay had immediate and understandable meaning for these peoples. In a very literal way, this is how these societies *were* created. The dust was turned to fields. Clay jars stored the food for life. If the immediacy of the metaphors seems old fashioned today, it is precisely because we no longer live like our ancestors. Some people say that religions of this period are on the wane because we no longer need to believe in them. But we might step back and ask—then what do we need to believe in now?

One new belief that has tried to take the place of religion in the old sense of the word is that of the belief in nature. Its politics has been called environmentalism. Since the early 1960s, this movement has attempted to call our collective attention to the destruction of the earth. Since this destruction is moving rapidly to a point where we are unsure of its long-term effects and whether or not they are reversible, environmentalism has become a fashionable way of thinking. Teenagers too have joined in. Like any political movement, as we shall see later on, environmentalism makes certain assumptions. The most important is that it says that all of us can, and should, become environmentalists. Our entire species' future is at stake. We all live on the same planet.

Fair enough. We *do* need to mind our manners with nature. But let's take a closer look at our collective relationship with nature before we leap headlong into the fashion. There are, no doubt, some secrets here as well that adults have been keeping to themselves. The first we already mentioned. We might have but thirty years left, according to one large study. But there is more to it than that. For the vast majority of humans' time on earth, we lived much closer to nature than today. This does not mean, as some environmentalists have thought, that we were closer in the sense of a compassionate intimacy. It merely meant that we did not have the high technology to insulate ourselves against the forces of nature. It did not mean that we did not want to be so insulated. Ancient peoples were *not* the first environmentalists. The stuff you hear from the native peoples around the world today, when it does address the problem of the environment, is recent. It's part of the very fashion that sparked a focused interest in the way in which small-scale societies lived and continue to try to live in rare regions of the world. Rather, these groups, sometimes with as few as fifty members, lived in a risky *competition* with nature. Questions like the following were the order of the day: "Will I get the plants I need, or will a snake bite me and kill me?" or "Will I hunt down the deer first, or will a puma get it and stop me from eating?" It was not, "Let me only take as much as I need so that the earth will continue to thrive."

The reason why small-scale groups in ancient times and in our own appear to be environmentally friendly is as simple as that—*they're small.* Their technology is not as intrusive as ours. The bow and arrow, the little trap, the spear, the net, all have very local effects on nature. The amount of food fifty people need to survive day to day in no way impinges on nature and the surrounding environment. Of course these cultures had rituals. The first paintings suggest that our ancient ancestors were trying to control the outcome of the hunt. When a group of men went out on the ocean to hunt a whale and bring it back, the women would stay on the beach and wait and pray. The prayers were addressed to the whale, and not to their mates. Or if one killed a deer, one would leave part of it for the puma out of respect for it as a hunter. The list goes on and on. Such rites may be found in all cultures of this scale and time period. But none of this has anything to do with the idea that nature was something that needed to be preserved. Rather, it was one's relationship with nature that needed to be forever balanced, for there was a deep awareness that nature was *dangerous.*

It comes out in the humor of ancient peoples and small groups today. The stories they told were about making fun of the very forces they feared. The jaguar was caricatured as an oafish moron, incapable of even the most basic intellectual tasks. He was always saved by a tiny bird, an insignificant animal in reality. The point of such joking narratives was not making fun *of* the reality, but to allay human anxiety *about* that very reality. It's no different if you have a teacher that you think you hate. And what teen doesn't? You and your friends sit around making fun of that person. This is often undeserved. But the structure of such stories is always that of an *inversion* of real relations. The reality is dangerous. Your teacher grades you and may even report you for discipline of some kind. They are the adults. You have to obey them to a certain extent. They influence your short-term future. But they're jerks. The jaguar is a little different. He's not a jerk, he's just *what* he is. He is an awesome competitor to the human hunter, far better equipped by instinct and physique to brave the dangers of the jungle. No human being can out-compete him directly. So we have to use our cunning and our technology—and our humor. Telling jokes and making fun of reality is one of the most ancient ways that humans coped with the awesome powers that surrounded them. This coping was more earthy back in the day because lives were much shorter and revolved around much the same things as did those of the animals: foraging, hunting, gathering, consuming, and reproducing. Even so, anthropologists have found that it is in these small-scale societies—the kind of societies *all* human beings lived in for millions of years—that there is the *most* leisure time. Amazingly, the amount of work these people do is by far the least. It is because they get what they need for the time being and that's it. Work day's over.

What a difference a few thousand years makes! *Here* is the source for the nostalgic yearning for nature. It is not directly about nature at all. The idea that nature reconnects with itself is too abstract to bring forth the action of a social movement like environmentalism. Like our ancestors and small-scale cousins, it is our relationship with nature that we are resentful about. We might even go so far to say that one of the motivations for killing native peoples around the world historically was that we hated the fact that they seemed to know what they were doing with nature. It was always such a struggle for us, from the beginning of herding and then farming on down to today. But these folks sat around the fire and sang songs all night, with seemingly no worry for the morrow. With their simple tools and weapons they had all they needed. Life was a breeze, unless a leopard leaped on you. The control of fire was no doubt a major step in the evolution of humanity. Animals of all kinds don't like it. They flee from it. We do too unless it is controlled. Fire is as dangerous an enemy as it always was, but only human can possess it. Myths of many cultures around the world celebrate this ability, from Prometheus the Greek culture-hero who steals the secret of fire from the gods and gives it to humankind, to Raven on the Pacific Northwest Coast of North America, who steals the sun and thus allows it to heat and light the ways of humans. These are two utterly unrelated cultures, and yet they speak the same language in their myths.

We humans need the sun and fire. We give meaning to these needs by thinking of how we, in the shadowy and deeply primordial days of our most ancient forebears, could have brought them to us. Such meanings are what we are. But they are culture, not nature. Nature was the obstacle to be overcome. It took a god to do it—Raven or Prometheus or whomever, it doesn't matter. We knew, from the outset, that if we were suddenly no longer part of nature, no longer *in* nature, we were going to need some help living *with* nature. Much later on, closer to our own time, it seemed as if we needed less and less. This is an error. One glance at our current situation will tell you that we need all the help we can get. And whatever gods may be out there, it also seems that we often only have ourselves to rely on. What then, is next?

Not very long ago, compared with the stuff we have been talking about, a reversal in our idea of nature took place.

This happened in direct reaction to industrialization and the rise of factory economies. Nostalgia for cultures that were different from our European one suddenly took center stage. Instead of feeling hatred toward our small-scale cousins, we felt admiration. Instead of trying to control nature and get it out of the way of our projects, we sought to preserve it. From the wildness of the English garden, fashionable in the seventeenth century—and in my hometown today—to the idea of having national parks, this new idea of nature had an effect. We tried, somewhat halfheartedly and with not anywhere near as much compassion, to 'preserve' native peoples as well. National parks and native reservations are very much the same thing. The difference is that animals and plants don't need our help. Other people, if we take away their means of life, all of a sudden are reliant upon us, even if they do not want to be. At the same time as we were romanticizing nature—that is, telling ourselves that nature was like a lover and we needed to love it—we continued its destruction apace. These new ideas had taken hold in the hearts and minds mostly of artists and philosophers, and not at all with regular people, much less manufacturers and politicians. Nature to them was the same old thing, something to be used or removed. Nature was either a tool or a waste.

And up until maybe the 1960s, the seeming vastness of nature—the endless forests, the depths of fossil fuels, all the fish in the sea—gave us the sense that nature could never be exhausted. It would always be there for us. No matter how many we became, no matter how inflated our needs were, nature could supply us. This is an idea that teenagers begin to question in another way. For this idea comes from the sense that children have about the abilities of their parents. Your dad and mom can do anything for you, at any time, for any need; they can satisfy it, from community, to love, to food, to warmth, shelter, and defense. Unless your family fell apart early on—lots do—only as a teenager do you begin to understand that the child's-eye view of parents is in fact grossly misleading. Your mom and dad can't do everything. There are things they shouldn't do. You need to find love and sex among your peers, for example. These too are very human needs. You need to make friends so that you can share experiences with people going through the same thing. Adults can help, but we have seen that we also can be a big obstacle to your self-understanding. So teens can easily grasp this problem of the environment, because you are presently coming to terms with similar problems in your human relationships.

But we can't understand it only as the opposition between experience and ignorance. Nature and society do have some kind of relationship with each other. The one is not the other's negation. What I mean by that is that nature does *not* represent the opposite of humanity. It is just different. When we see aliens in film and television, we know that they actually represent something about us. When we use images of animals or cartoons of them in kid's films, we are also talking about ourselves. A real alien, when and if we encounter one, will have *no* such relationship to us. It is not an opposite. It is different. Indeed, one might say that an authentic genuine alien *is* difference itself. That is, such a being would be so different from us that we would have to work hard to understand what it was and how it communicated. Popular science fiction and fantasy films are not about understanding *this* kind of difference. In the same way, *environmentalism is not really about nature.* People who are concerned about the environment are concerned about human beings.

It has to be this way. If it were otherwise, then there would be another, perhaps even greater problem. Think about it another way, through the people who love pets or animals in general. We get a clue to the negative potential of environmentalism through some of them. You or I might be like them. You see bumper stickers that say, "The more people I meet, the more I like my cat (or dog, etc.)." Okay, I can understand that. People are tough and often untrustworthy. They might be unreliable even when they are honest. A dog you can count on—man's best friend, and all that. And if cats

appear not to really need us, they at least are low mainte-
nance. Dogs have a historical advantage over cats. We have
been living with them for about ten millennia longer. So it's
no surprise that they love us and need us, and cats seem to
simply use us, more or less. I am not talking about this to
favor one animal over another. The point is, if we go too far
down the road of loving nature, we tend to depart from loving each other. The bumper sticker, however sarcastic, and
whatever grain of truth may be in it, is a step down this other
road. This road we cannot afford to take. It is one thing to
use pets as therapy to get us back into trusting relationships
with other humans. It is quite another to use pets as *substitute* humans. You have all heard of 'cat ladies' or similar
people who have long since given up on any meaningful human relationships. It is very sad, but they may have found
themselves more like the animals they live with. In fact, we
could say that all pet relationships are pet therapy. But sometimes the therapy does not work.

When it does, domesticated animals—as opposed to wild
animals—are great to have around. If we do not have children,
we might have pets instead. But children are not pets, and pets
are not children. I have often seen people who make errors
both ways. Dogs and cats began their lives with humans as
tools. They were extremely useful. Dogs were used for herding from about twenty thousand years ago. Cats were used for
rodent killing when farming came along about ten thousand
years later. Birds were used for hunting and for sending messages. Snakes were for keeping down vermin in gardens. People even used larger spiders in the home for eating all the other
bugs. When I lived in Mississippi, a place where there are lots
and lots of little creatures everywhere, I had a king snake in
my backyard and what locals called a kitchen spider in my
house. I never had a problem with pests inside or outside. But
the snake and spider were not my pets, either! They simply
hung out doing what their species did. It benefits humans to
have certain kinds of wild animals around too, though they
tend to be the smaller ones. Animals have, in short, helped

us to get where we are today. We can respect that, however, without turning them into surrogate human beings. This is the key error of the environmental movement and of some of its politics. *It turns nature into part of human nature.*

If you have sometimes thought, as I have, that some people who go on about the environment are forgetting something important, I would agree. In a less important way, they forget that there is a difference between pets and pests. More importantly, they forget that anything we do in the name of nature we do for ourselves. We do not need to save nature. We need to save ourselves. This also means saving ourselves from aspects of *our* human nature that are destructive. We also need to protect ourselves from natural forces that are also destructive. In doing so, we alter the course of what nature would do if left alone. We cannot help but do this. Sure, we can set aside large tracts of land and ocean to try to keep them more or less in a wild state. But increasingly this means less and less. In another place I lived, in South-Central British Columbia in Canada, forty-four bears were killed in a single summer. These bears had wandered into town, started eating garbage, and went a little nuts. Forty-four seems like a lot of bears to me over four months. This does have some tragedy about it. But unless we want to radically alter how and where we live, this kind of problem will keep happening. To alter human living in order to preserve some version of nature that has already been altered radically over time is questionable. It may be better to help nature do its own thing in select regions, and then alter it to serve us in others. We might even be able to keep the two kinds of places apart from one another. But the purpose of this would only be to hedge our bets with the planet in general. If some plague or other catastrophe wipes out the human species, there would be other species left to carry on life on earth. *This* kind of care for the environment makes sense. But the idea that human beings must *love* nature and try to avoid stepping on its toes carries us into the fog of forgetting our primary duties to our fellow human beings.

As with all political causes, as we will see in a bit, the environmental movement also has attracted people who *need* a cause to make their own lives worthwhile. These people should be avoided at all costs. They tend toward fanaticism and dogmatism. That is, if you don't agree with them you're wrong. That's it. All of you probably know people like that. But as teens, the issues are mostly about stuff that could better be called *opinions* than causes. Like, who is the best drummer or the hottest singer? Who is going to win the Super Bowl or what fashion is the coolest? Stuff like that. Not that you can't think about serious issues. You are just fed these fake issues to think about by adults so that you are not more of a nuisance to adults than you already are.

But in the politics of nature, sometimes the lowest urges of human nature come out. So a dogmatist is someone who not only has made up his mind, they tend to be interested only in others that think like them. Since the environment really *is* a serious issue, perhaps the most serious of our time, then these kinds of people become particularly dangerous. So what can the rest of do to avoid this, while at the same time avoiding the destruction of the earth?

Start out by making a distinction between nature and human beings. Nature does not want or need anything. It certainly doesn't need us. The planet would no doubt be better off without any humans in terms of the suffering of animal life, for instance, and the poisoning of oceans, lakes, and rivers, and the laying waste to the earth. Keeping this distinction in mind, then try asking what human beings need to survive as a *whole* species, not just your group or mine, not just teenagers or adults, or men or women. Think about the amount of stuff you really need. Think about all the stuff you can keep and for how long. Think about buying items, even large ones like cars that can last a very long time. Good vehicles kept up well can last up to thirty years or more. Think about how many children you might give birth to, and how many you might adopt. The new 'three-R's' motto of the applied environmental movement is in fact a good practical rule to use: reduce, re-use, recycle. Think about where you might work and if you can get there without a vehicle. Even simple things like having a shower versus a bath help out. Nature is a grand stage that human beings have only walked on for a very short time. It will go on without us as long as we care for ourselves first.

Since the environment and its future could be the number-one challenge that comes out of the more important challenges of human conflicts, lifestyle, and the economy, one might think it would get a perfect score. But the confusion surrounding ideas of nature and the serious problem of people who turn away from their fellow human beings to fight for an anonymous set of forces suggest a slightly lower score of eight out of ten.

7. The Secrets of Politics (and family)

〰〰〰〰〰〰〰〰〰〰〰〰〰〰〰〰〰〰〰〰〰〰

It would be nice to simply say, politics, bad; family, good. But as always, things are a little more complex. We have already seen that certain things in the family may be very dangerous for teens and younger children. The family, too, has its politics. It is much more real for teens than are politicians who claim that everyone is part of one big happy family. But in general I would like to suggest that politics brings out the worst in us, and family brings out the best. How is this so?

In our modern society, politics gives the opportunity to hold a vast amount of power. Power in the family may be wielded gently or punitively, as we have seen. But power in politics is of a different magnitude. It tends to be only effective when wielded forcefully, even to the point of evil. Politicians, elected or not, either go in for this career with the idea that they can serve the community or control it. Power is something that is either forced upon us or is sought after. People who fit in the first category are usually benign politicians. They have a sense that they can perform a civic duty. They may even want to alter things so that life gets better for more people.

But persons who hear the second call, that of power as a weapon, are dangerous. To support them is always to court disaster. The trouble is, until these people are in office, until they officially have access to political power, we are often unsure as to their motives. Indeed, we are not so stupid to fall for people who out and out show themselves as power hungry *before* they assume office. We are rightly suspicious of these people. If they expose themselves too soon, they will usually get no further.

In times of crisis though, like the decades leading up to World War Two in Germany, people become very forgiving of those who actually seek power. We say, "He sounds like a madman, but he will be good for us because he can get things done." This 'getting things done' phrase is a dangerous one. It suggests that we are frustrated by inaction or the normal political process. Or maybe things aren't going our way. The stuff we would like to see put in place isn't happening. How many times have I heard people in my walk of life talk this way? They want to either seek power and control themselves or help someone they like to do so. All of them, once in control, act as if they have the right to do what they see fit. Elected dogmatists—remember, this just means people who think they are right and don't listen to others—are worse dictators than those who seize power by other means. They can use the excuse that they were, after all, elected. One of the two worst mass dictators in history was elected. "The people have spoken," they utter ominously.

Well, it is true that we regular folks get frustrated by the way things are. Most of us take it out on you guys, in the home. But some plot and plan in the public realm. When they are successful in wresting power away from those they hate, they turn around and act just like them.

The pull of politics is always the same. If one is drawn to it, one needs to immediately take a step back. We should always be asking ourselves: "Why am I taken with this idea? Why am I convinced that I could do a better job than those who are working right now? Why are my ideas better than theirs? Are my ethics up to the task, and where is the proof of this?" These questions and many other related ones should be in the heads of public servants on most days. Let's look at that much abused title—'public servant.' It should be taken quite literally. Even me as a professor at a publicly funded university fits this category. We often, however, seem to be working for ourselves. Indeed, this book falls into the academic category of 'service to the community.' It's the scholar's version of helping out like big brothers or sisters, for instance. If you are only interested in serving yourself, you should go into the private sector. But even this isn't quite fair. For most large corporations and their leaders contribute a huge amount of time and money to the wider community and encourage their workers to do so as well. Even small businesses do something in this regard.

The idea that public is public and private is private has broken down over the years. In a strange way, the Internet may be seen as the hallmark of this new, mixed space. You are often both private and public at the same time when you are online. So while serving the community may take many forms, being part of the community does too.

But of course pure self-interest remains a large factor in modern political and business life. We might accuse both arenas of merely drumming up support for their schemes when they hand wealth to charity or designate funds for health or education. We are also not so stupid to think that there is any such thing as a simple gift. Everything has strings attached. From the aid we give to other countries—we want them to do what we tell them to do—all the way down to the allowances you get from your parents—same thing. So we neither expect nor believe in charity for its own sake. Something else is at stake. Finding out what it is may be important. Sometimes we find out later on that it is something we would not have supported. But by then it is often too late. The self-interest of those controlling the situation by making offers and gifts to us has shown itself to be exactly what it is.

So we are left with a potential mess. Once in power, dictators are notoriously hard to remove. From wicked stepparents (a stereotype) to ruthless dictators (*not*, unfortunately, a stereotype), the sense that they have *arrived* is strong. They fought hard to gain control, and they will never give it up without a tremendous fight. It is far easier to prevent dictatorship than to get rid of it once it occurs. So in *democratic* societies—those with political systems where one must appeal to large numbers of people to gain power—we try to control the would-be controllers before they are in control. The pursuit of power for its own sake is one of our worst habits as contemporary human beings. We must be alert to the possibility of its abuse. In fact, we don't think that abuse is just possible, but likely. Sometimes we can see ahead that this or that candidate will likely abuse power. Once again, the basis for all of this is happening to you as teenagers right now.

Think about the many examples of when your parents decide to let you have more control over your life: your first pet, your first time home alone, first use of their cars, first car, first time alone with a prospective partner, first part-time job. The list goes on and on. It does seem kind of pathetic when you look back at its stages. For me, the first time I got a chemistry set led to a series of disasters. But this was coupled with the first home alone. Bad combination. Way worse than my driving or my attempts to have sex. But my parents were apparently oblivious to all but the most odd combinations of firsts. I saved my house from blowing up and my parents never got the slightest wind of it. But when a visitor from a different city whom I didn't know from Adam got drunk at a party that I was not at and barfed all over my bedroom at 4 a.m., I didn't see my girlfriend for a week. What did those things have to do with each other? In the same way, adults of all kinds strain to figure out what *our* peers are up to. But instead of the bedroom, the lonely road, or the home laboratory, it is politics that draws our attention.

And inattention, because in democracies about half of us don't seem to care at all what the politicians are doing, or who they are, or where they are coming from, or where they are taking us. We don't vote. We don't rally. We don't complain in public venues, like newspapers and radio. Once again, the Internet has been a big help to the problem of apathy, referring to the uncaring character of the political community, which is us. We are notoriously apathetic about politics. In part, we know that politicians don't listen to most of us. We also know that in our modern democracy there are forces at work that undermine its sincerity. Special people and special groups abound. These people and their groups have more power than the rest of us. We find it hard to compete with them. They influence politics at a higher level than us. The rules seem to be made for them. Often the rules are actually made *by* them. What can we do about it? We are small; they are big. We are poor; they are rich, and so on.

Even if we represent the great mass of society, we often feel we are outnumbered by people with power. And power seeks, more than anything else, to simply reproduce itself. It does so sometimes by getting bigger and sometimes by focusing its energies into specific areas of importance. Governments, and thus real people, follow along with this. Each political regime that gets in seeks to reproduce its electoral results next time. We know that governments and politicians will try anything to reinstate themselves. Knowing this does not immediately put us at an advantage, but it might if we use it correctly. They want us to vote for them, well, here's what we want from them. Why do we not do this? Here's the secret: aside from promises, promises, which are often not kept when these folks get power again, the key to political reproduction is built into a system that *tells us what we want ahead of time.*

Think once again about your first car or date. You already have a strong feeling about what you want from them— freedom and pleasure. But where do these feelings come from? We're not born with them. They don't automatically turn on as soon as you hit age fourteen or so. No, adults and teens are influenced to a great degree by what their peers are thinking and doing. This much is obvious. There are no secrets here per se. The secret lies behind the actual stuff you want. No specific thing is that important. But the idea that you shouldn't make up your own minds is. "Too much thinking and the world will fall apart." This is one of the biggest lies all of us are told and then keep telling ourselves. "Change is too scary to take in all at once, so any change should be avoided." Another lie, to a point.

Change *is* scary for many of us, especially for adults. You might think that we are used to it, and that it's teenagers who have anxieties about it. The opposite is generally truer. Teens seek change. After all, you want to see yourself move on. But adults get stuck in ruts very easily. We've already had enough change, commotion, and upheaval in our lives. So *we* seek security.

And a big part of this security we are looking for comes from the unchanging landscape of modern politics. Even I have counseled you against revolution. But change itself is always happening. It does not mean extremes. The world goes on without us if we don't change and adapt. Yes, it is difficult, way more so for adults than teenagers. The hardest thing about it is to know when to make a change and when to stick to your guns. This decision must sometimes be made on a daily basis. But often enough it is relatively trivial. Every four or five years or so, depending on where you live, we are asked if we want to make a change in government. Sometimes we do. But we also have noted that, over time, the choices that we are given look very much the same. This makes sense. We might be willing to change a little, but not a lot. If two or more political parties look almost the same, we don't have to worry about making a wrong choice.

We sometimes complain about the lack of real political choice. But after all, you can't blame the politicians. They are catering to what they see as our wants. And we don't want radical shifts in power every few years. We look around the world and see people in other countries suffering greatly precisely because of these kinds of shifts. So maybe a little boredom is better. The problem with the lack of political choices, especially at the highest levels, is that politicians don't have to work very hard to get our consent. They take us for granted. Once in power, they basically ignore us. It is often too late to change them out, at least for a while. So because we don't want too much excitement—we see its results elsewhere—what we get is boredom and a kind of gentle arrogance. Boredom leads to apathy. Arrogance leads to distrust. And apathy and distrust are the two chief characteristics of our political life.

We live in large and increasingly diverse societies. We know who votes for whom. There are long-term general trends that politicians and their managers follow closely. Appeals are made to specific groups: lower taxes for the middle classes, tax breaks for the wealthy, roads for suburban residents, not much for the poor, whether rural or urban. If our nation is a world player, then a lot of time and effort goes into keeping up our international status. The issues on the home front can be glossed over. Most people don't care much for international politics. Take care of your own first is the common refrain. To a great extent this is good advice, both in politics and in the family. Another bumper sticker: "Focus on your own darn family," states the case concisely. But because we are large and diverse, no single political party, much less a single politician, can provide for all of our wants. So they take the middle road, attracting the most voters for the least effort. Everyone wants less taxes. But not everyone needs more services. The wealthy can fend for themselves. They are content to do so as long as they have the money, some of it from less taxes, to pay for private services. The poor already know that politicians don't work for them, and neither does the system as a whole. Most of us, in the middle, are squeezed both ways. It is interesting that in North America, neither the poor nor the wealthy vote in large numbers. Why? The poor have given up. No one really represents their interests anyways. And the wealthy know that whoever is in power, the basics of the system won't change. They will always be at the top, so why bother voting?

This alone explains much voter apathy. The middle votes, but we are only about two-thirds of the population. So most of us vote, but the two ends don't. We are squeezed symbolically as well as materially. We don't trust the wealthy, so we try not to vote for stuff that benefits them alone. But we also think the poor are at fault for being poor. We often say to ourselves, "I work; why can't they?" Working isn't easy.

Maybe it is more fun not to work and just have others pay your way. But, of course, it isn't fun to be poor. Not at all. We deep down know this, whatever nasty things we might say about poor people. We work precisely because we *don't* want to be like them. Most of us could care less about real wealth. The people who have it either aren't nice people, so we think, or they work *too* much. We saw that much at least in a previous chapter. So the people who vote do care about the issues. We just don't know if we can trust anyone to pick them up for us once they are in power. We hope they do, and sometimes some things do work out for the middle class. If we are in a charitable mood and if our own economies are good, then we even take care of the poor a little too. But if the economy is bad, if more of us are heading in a downward direction, we cut the poor off in a trice. We also direct more of our complaints against the rich. It sometimes works.

Lately, in the USA, some of the wealthiest people in the world have banded together and given much of their wealth over to various charities and foundations. It's a massive amount of private money we are talking about. It far outshines the public funds going in those directions. These people aren't communists. They are the most successful capitalists of all time. They have taken philanthropy, the act of sharing wealth voluntarily, to a new height. Individuals are currently doing far more than governments about poverty and inequality.

Good for them. But one thing to remember: It doesn't change the *structure* of the system. This is one of the points of being generous as an individual. We don't have to lose anything. At the same time, we can also hang our hats on the sound historical sensibility that radical revolutions cause more suffering than they are worth. So far, so good. But giving money away to existing organizations that are already part of the existing system is only a first step. One could do more politically. One could fund a new party that acts on behalf of the poor. One could lobby to change the tax laws or to reserve a certain part of the tax income for people who need it. None of this is revolutionary. It eases the burden of our economic system for those who suffer under it the most. This is the kind of politics we need, and as adults, you'd think we'd be compassionate enough to fight for it. But we seem to have too many of our own things to worry about. We resent the poor because we are scared we might become like them. We resent the rich because we know we will never become like them. It's fear on one side and sour grapes on the other. Not much wisdom to be found in politics like these. But these are the ultimate foundations of middle-class attitudes toward politics and other people in our society.

So while we hope for better times ahead, we also prepare for more of the same. In doing so, we cater to the politicians' own brand of uncaring. We don't expect much from them, so they don't give much. Sound familiar? Parenting manuals of all stripes tell adults the same thing about teenagers. If we don't expect much from you, you won't give much. We are told that we must gradually increase age-appropriate responsibilities in your direction. You need to take them on, because that is the primary way you become like us.

So we see that the manner in which we act politically can often be found in the family. Not that politicians are usually friends or family. They usually hail from privileged parts of society. We don't know the people they know and never will. But we think we know them because they are in the media all the time. We begin to feel like they are real people, like us. We want to give them a break. We treat them harshly, sometimes, but at the end of the day, we also know they are going to leave us alone. They are eventually out of office. All this too should sound immediately familiar. We get to know you guys as our kids. We cut you some slack, sometimes treat you harshly. And in the end, we feel bad or at least nostalgic because you eventually disappear from the household. Teenagers and politicians have similar relationships to the rest of us.

The politics of being a teenager is a response to this. Your parents are being jerks; you shut down. Voters are critical;

politicians back off. Your parents reward you; you respond. Voters show support; politicians cater to them. Nothing much in this. It should be obvious that people, at whatever level, are responding either positively or negatively to the same sets of circumstances that we all grew up in. A truly alien politician will never be found. A teen who doesn't act like one will be questioned. Even if you're the best kid around and you're fifteen, your parents will wonder what the heck is going on if you never act out. No one, in other words, is incorruptible.

A famous historian once said that power and corruption were inevitably intertwined. The one leads to the other—the more of one, the more of the other. And we certainly are aware that politicians can be very corrupt, from the small-town mayor to the president or prime minister. Just because everyone has their price—and excellent people on their way to their heaven have this as their price—does not mean that we can be bought. The two phrases are not in an identity relation with one another. This just means that they do not mean, or have to mean, the same thing. We can resist our own asking price. In fact, we need to be able to do this in order to become mature and decent human beings.

Take a common case for teens: you see someone else's lover at school. "My god, she/he is *soooo* hot," you say to yourself. You want them. You're with someone else, or no one. It is part of the adolescent experience that romantic relationships are almost always short term. Sure, we hear of a few high school sweethearts getting married and dying together. But that is why we hear of those cases—they are news. At your stage of the game, you can trade partners and dance with little effort. Once you are adults, it takes a lot more work. And very often—in fact, about half the time—it takes dishonesty. In other words, it takes a form of *corruption* to get what you think you want—someone else's spouse, or someone single when you're not. It's all the same.

Indeed, the most common form of corruption in the family setting is adultery, or cheating. It's more common even than people hitting their kids, so far as we know. While child abuse is likely underreported, one would think that cheating would be too. Except it's oddly not seen as such. Adults can brag about how many people they've laid, just like teens do. The other interesting thing is that women now cheat as often as men.

This is because of the changes for women with regard to work. Women cheat as often as men now because they can afford it. Nothing more. If your husband doesn't like it, well, see you later! Same thing that men always did to women. Great, someone might say, we're finally getting even. But like drugs, just because its equal opportunity does not make it healthy or right. It's still wrong no matter how many people engage in it.

Same with politicians. Every world leader (with a few exceptions) is corrupt in some way. They are cheating, not on their spouses, but on their citizens. So our leader has to be that way too? Hardly. But it is ultimately our fault if we elect someone whom we cannot trust and then complain about it as if we didn't suspect him in the first place. We should know better by now.

In this way, politics is actually much more transparent than is marriage. People change over the life course. We fall in and out of love. We fall in and out of love with someone other than our spouse. We want our spouses back. They want us back, or not. But when we take vows, our own small version of the oath of political office, we at least do tend to believe in them at the time. The statistics say that about half of marriages end in divorce. What this doesn't tell you is that if you marry before you're twenty-five, you have an eighty-five percent chance of getting divorced! So as a teen, don't be in any hurry to marry. At least wait until thirty or so when the odds even out. That is, thirty-year-olds will only divorce about half the time.

While this may not be inspiring, it is better to be realistic. Realism is a form of honesty. As such, it is the opposite of corruption. One needs to be realistic even about one's honesty. Because I work with people not much older than you, I have had over the years a great many chances to cheat on the person I have been with. I've never done it. Partly because I was worried about how *I* would feel about it later. I didn't want to have to deal with my bad conscience. I was also stung with the sense that I could hurt someone else's feelings. Or at least, I *hoped* I would be. Indeed, for some of the persons I was with I might not have hurt them at all. If this were the case, then I had to make my decision on principle alone. *This* kind of honesty involves in its turn a kind of vanity. Because it says to me, "I am more holy than thou; I would never do such a thing." Even honesty has sources that are not always the best. But when these sources come together in a certain way, their *results* are better.

Same with realism in politics. Any honest person getting into public life knows how it works. They may have to connive, cajole, and cater to interests they don't personally share. They will have to cut other people out who are dragging them down. They become like the system itself. But a few of these people, in spite of the work it takes to reach the top, preserve their honesty and use it to reinforce their realism. They stay real. To do so is not to think that people around you are honest. It's more honest to think that they may not be. We cannot afford to be suspicious of our spouses on a daily basis. We need to trust them in a way we do not need to trust our politicians. This means that politics is in fact an easier thing than family. We can actually ask politicians to *demonstrate* their honesty to us. To do so to your mate would be at best insulting. In fact, politicians are in the business of either demonstrating such honesty or covering up the fact they do not have it. Most of them do a little of both in their motley careers. Most of them are practical minded. They do not live on ideals alone. You can't do that in the public life any more than you can do that in marriage. But in family life, we want to act according to our ideals and try to live up to them. In political life, not so much. The forces ranged against politicians are often too strong for any one person to cope with. Politics has the reputation for sleaze not because only sleazy people are attracted to it. This stereotype is unfair. It's the same as any other line of work. The problem is the overall way in which we live around the world. The idea of competing nation-states and competing citizens makes our fellow human being into an enemy, a threat. Instead, we need to think about getting together in a big way. A world that really means *a* world, with everyone aware that the other has needs too.

One way we can start to move in that direction involves you. Simply, we need to drop the voting age to thirteen. Teens are always asking annoying questions. There is no more relevant place to ask such questions than in politics. If politicians as adults had to answer to you as well as their peers, things would start to change. You guys are not jaded like we are. You embrace change rather than fear it. You've still got some creativity and curiosity left over from the menace of schooling and dimwitted and trivial media. You want to know why things are the way they are, and not so you can just sit back and enjoy them. Even teens get bored with too much downtime. Teenagers like action. They want to hear how problems can be solved and not just avoided. We need you to breathe new life into our political system. In fact, the reason why you can't vote now is *because* of all of this. We have already seen that adults have a vested interest in keeping things the way they are. We've survived and made it. Why should things be easier for you? Why should we change the world we fought to get into just because our kids don't like it?

All these selfish rationales are accompanied by another dirty secret. After the various modern political revolutions, there were ongoing fights about who should be able to vote. In the USA, it was originally decided that just white men who owned property—including slaves—should be able to vote. These people were the 'best' citizens. If it had stayed like that, 1776 would have been nothing more than a bad joke. But gradually, through heated arguments and even a civil war, the franchise was extended to all adult men without regard to social position or race. Even native people were able to vote by the mid-twentieth century. Even women by the 1920s.

The secret that is revealed by looking back historically is that *the same arguments that were used to keep non-whites and women from voting then are used to keep you from voting today.* Exactly the same: kids are irrational; they don't know enough about the world to participate in politics; we shouldn't have to answer to our kids, they are worth less than us; they aren't as mature; they will only vote the way their parents vote anyway, and so on. While some of this may be true for an eight-year-old, none of it is so for teenagers. You are perfectly capable, with a little self-study, of voting in as serious a manner as any adult. In fact, one would hope you'd be a lot *more* serious than many of us! Blacks and women had to study up on the political process to participate in it. So can teens. There is no difference, I repeat, *no* difference between the historical arguments we now cringe at and the current arguments we swear by. Talk about hypocrisy, especially if it is your mom or, if you are non-white, your parents who tell you that you shouldn't be able to participate in the political process. Next time anyone does that, nail them to a cross.

If someone who looks like me says it, then it's just the same old thing white guys have been saying to everyone for about five hundred years: "We're better than you and that's too bad, ain't it?" No real hypocrisy there. We are just being true to our roots. There is still no argument, but at least we're being honest. This time, the weightier shoe is on the female and non-white foot. *Those* adults should be helping you guys get the vote. *They* should be helping you study up. Then what white guys say wouldn't matter anyway.

So start agitating. Start asking why you are cut out of a process that affects you just as much as us. For example, as we will shortly see, modern wars don't discriminate in their victims. It's governments that make war, not soldiers.

Governments we elect. I bet there would be less war if teens had the vote, but of course I may be wrong. In any case, you want to stop being just part of the problem in our eyes. You can help us out in a big way here. And if we stand in your way, don't lose heart.

Because politics is full of corruption, because people who seek power over others are attracted to it more than other careers, and because politics pits nations and people against one another, one would think it would be universally a bad thing. But politics is how we take care of ourselves, too. It represents ideals more than actual people, yes, but those ideals are worth working for. Because of this odd mixture, and because we need to be much more interested in politics than we are, I am going to rate it a surprising four out of ten.

8. The Secrets of War (and peace)

~~~~~~

This chapter would seem like a no-brainer. Remind people of what war does to us, give it a big fat zero, and move on. Not a chance. We need to know about the very thing we fear the most. We need to take a good look at it, however briefly. We need to take note of its biggest threat: that when we stare at it, it stares back at us. It's like looking into the eyes of the devil. We can easily become the monster it creates. And we have done so many times. Let's find out how this works.

First of all, we might ask why there is war. There are a number of reasons. But these reasons are masked by rationalizations. The biggest error is suggesting that religion is a root cause of war. This may have sometimes been so in the past, but not today. Religion is used by various leaders as both an excuse to go to war and a way to get people to go to war. That is, we say that our sacred beliefs are being threatened. And then we say that if we do not defend them we are not true believers. To be cast out in this way is to effectively lose your community. So we have to go. We might get killed, but our deaths are honorable. To be cast out ahead of time is to die a dishonorable death. But what lays behind the rhetoric of the use of religion are other sources of conflict which make more sense.

If you question people in a serious way, very few care what other people believe about unearthly things. Their practical relevance is itself questionable. Only fanatics worry about such things. And today, fortunately, the era of religious fanaticism is, for the most part, on the wane. Religion remains as an excuse and rationale for getting certain people to sacrifice themselves for another, muted, cause. This is especially, though not exclusively, the case in the Middle East in our time.

The real causes of war have to do with competition for resources and control over others. We have already mentioned that our world today is composed of nation-states in competition with one another. All alliances are practical ones. There may be some underlying sentiment, as there is among English-speaking countries because of the former British Empire, but this sentiment is of the same cloth as religion. It holds no real power over us. It may help persuade us to do the unthinkable—king and country, or God is on our side, that sort of thing—but it has no ultimate force.

The ultimatum citizens are given in times of crisis has more to do with the law and life and limb. We might be put in prison for not fighting for our countries and suffer other social stigma—a negative sanction or mark—as well. If the crisis comes home to us we could be killed by the enemy. We are not so much fighting to save our country as our culture and society, as well as our lives. *These* factors are the real ones.

At a personal level, we don't care what other people believe about religion. We don't care if our country is the most powerful. We don't care if elites hold on to their wealth or not. On a darker note, we also tend not to care if *other* people's children are getting killed. What we care about is what might happen if we lose. We think, sometimes rightly, that everything we now know will be changed for the worse.

Cultures have always been suspicious of one another. Like I said before, early small-scale societies did not love one another any more than we do. It's just that they could never get the better of one another. All societies had the same structure, and all were small. But with the start of herding and farming, things began to change. In particular, these two newer modes of existence didn't get along. The herders, nomadic and highly mobile, were like a massive cavalry to the infantry of the slow-paced farmers.

In Asia in particular, millennia of wars took place between these kinds of groups. Often, as was the case in China, the mobile people settled down after conquering the sedentary people, that is, those who stayed in the same place and grew their crops year after year. The former herders became like the farmers after ruling over them for a few centuries. In this way, the culture that originally lost absorbed their conquerors and in this way ended up winning in the end. This pattern repeated itself in India, Persia, and the Near East time after time. Finally, in Europe, the Roman Empire fell in this way to mobile conquerors coming out of Russia and the North. But in the end, it was the Roman culture, now Christianized, which triumphed as the northern groups were pacified and converted. This culture in turn reacted with violence against the rise of Islam. The original Muslims were highly mobile and had a military advantage over the Mediterranean groups. In but a century, they conquered from the Middle East all the way to central France.

Islam is sometimes called the religion of the sword. But this isn't quite fair. Muslims did not generally force conversions upon those they conquered. For most people, one religion was pretty much like the other. Especially the three so-called religions of Abraham: Judaism, Christianity, and Islam.

Most converts were willing and practical. If these were the new rulers, we might as well 'do as the Romans do' and get along. An odd and obscure historical secret about this time is that the original Muslims were pissed off that the Christians were not following the true teachings of Jesus in the Levant, and so attacked them to push them to be more authentic in their beliefs. The three Abrahamic religions *are* related of course, which makes all of the conflicts among them all the more tragically ironic. Yet even during these times, religion was used as an excuse to get people to defend their wider interests. Their entire way of life was more important than any single part of it. Religion cannot, and should not, be separated from culture. This has occurred precisely because unscrupulous people want to use religion as a weapon.

Beyond this, however, are the more fundamental differences of language, subsistence, making a living, social organization patterns such as kinship, and the ways in which
people cope with loss or celebrate joy. These differences are
deeper than those of any revealed religion.

For now, it is enough to say that religion is used as a rationalization for violence only as much as it is used for the
opposite. The fact that different cultures did not get along
historically should tell us all we need to know. Their conflicts were about competition for resources, land, territorial
dominance, and the ability to enforce or enhance the security of their dominion. No different than our own time. Not
only did conquest allow you to assert your power over others
who may have been a threat, it also insulated you against
threats farther afield. An enemy would have to travel across
thousands of miles to get to your home, passing through the
homes of many others you had already made part of your
empire. The conquerors usually didn't enforce their own culture on others. Indeed, most of those who conquered felt im-
measurably superior to those they vanquished. The Nazis'
attitudes were modeled on certain ancient sources. The Slavs
were not to be made German, nor were the Jews. They were
seen as by nature incapable of rising to this station. German-
hood, Aryan supremacy, was for Northern Europeans only.

Certainly if you resisted the conquest you would be killed.
But death is not conversion. If you didn't resist you would
be more or less ignored, as with the Islamic conquests. The
Greeks, however, killed everyone off. Dead people cannot
rise again to take revenge. The Nazis borrowed *this* model
and applied it in the most systematic and ruthless manner
history had ever seen.

The main problem of competition for resources, space,
and security is made worse by the problem of language. Our
myths speak to our sensitivity about this issue. The Tower
of Babel, for one, suggests that humans wanted to understand one another. But to be able to do so would have made
us like the gods, so Babel was destroyed, partly by lack

of cooperation, and partly by the jealously guarded omniscience of God.

The diversity of thousands of languages makes cross-cultural communication a huge challenge. But we have some evidence that communication was also present along with fighting even between early, small-scale social groups. The key was not to tread on each other's toes. Live and let live was an early motto of humankind. In Australia, for instance, different social groups invented incredibly sophisticated ways of intermarrying. This was done to share scarce resources and keep different groups friendly. They also invented an entire belief system centered on the sharing of certain kinds of foods and spaces, and the taboo, or making something forbidden, around others. One group's food became the next group's sacred animal, and so on. In this way, everyone had enough to survive. This ingenious system was shattered by the arrival of the Europeans.

Which points up another major source of war: When two entirely different cultural and political systems encounter one another, there is usually conflict. The more organized and larger system almost always wins. Any exception to this historic trend is based on the rottenness of the core of the larger society—Ancient Rome, for example—or the lack of political will and economic investment on the part of the more powerful—present-day Afghanistan is an example.

The civil war in the United States was of course not about freeing black slaves. Emancipation was offered up by the North in the hopes that the slaves would rebel against their masters. The promise was kept by the victors mainly because slaves were not useful in the northern economic system. It was this system, industrial capitalism, that triumphed over an outmoded one, slave-based farming. The conflict was about two economic and technological systems that could not exist side by side. This is the reality about the world being too small for the both of us.

This idea has often been faked as well, of course. The Nazis were the most offensive in this way, saying to other groups that the world was not big enough for both of them to live in. The Nazis said they needed more living space.

But the idea of insulating one's security by having vast amounts of land stretching outward from the core areas of your home was not by any means a Nazi invention. All nation-states, if they are competing on the worldwide stage, attempt to do this. Oceans are the best way. These vast stretches of territory insulate against attack. Even countries with long-range missiles might not be able to reach us, as is the case with China today if we are living in certain parts of North America. Oceans and airspace are patrolled by submarines and satellites, reaching out their security tentacles far beyond the scope of earlier societies. It is costly, no doubt. But it is less costly than actual war. Warfare with the goal of increasing one's territory is an ancient manner of enhancing one's security. If two different economic systems are involved, the more industrial one usually wins. This is so simply due to the ability to mass-produce higher technologies and get them to the war zone faster. The Franco-Prussian war of 1870-71 issued a German victory due to rail transport. Rail was also consequential in the US Civil War. Railways are a hallmark of industrial societies, not farming or herding. Cavalry is okay. Tanks, sometimes called armored cavalry, are better.

In spite of our suspicions of others and our immediate inability to understand what they are saying to us, war is not inevitable. We usually try to see what the other side wants before we fight them. If they want something we cannot give up and they won't give up their desires, fighting is likely. But just as often, small-scale groups found a way around this by offering other stuff to the opposing group in exchange. Trade alliances, sometimes spreading out thousands of miles, also developed. Sometimes these were enforced by warfare, but just as often there was symbolic reinforcement of them. To break them would be to risk conflict. New languages developed among trading partners. These tongues had versions of common words made up of sounds found in more than one language. Through these trading languages, you could communicate with people you had never seen or heard of before. It is an ancient lesson that it is almost always better to use peaceful means to get what you need or want. Peace is, at the very least, cheaper than war. Modern war is bad for most commerce. Arms dealers aside, warfare wrecks economies and plunges nations into debt. Loss of labor power is another issue. Recovering economies in Europe after 1945 had hardly anyone to work in them. Trade is also a form of competition. Who can get the best deal? But it is at least civil, if not entirely friendly. It is an outlet for security and peace of mind. A regular trading partner is seldom a threat and even less seldom an outright enemy.

Teenagers can easily get a sense of what it would have been like to meet someone for the first time with a view to marrying them. Ancient societies, and small-scale groups into our own time, often intermarried with neighboring groups. It did not matter if you spoke the same language. Languages can be learned, even by adults. Your awkward moments during first dates—and there is always at least one of these moments—are testament that even people who think they are basically the same are not. You adapt and compromise. If you want a second date, you have to. No different between cultures. And it should be no different among contemporary countries. The fact that we selfishly and sometimes blindly think we should be able to have everything we want in spite of the presence of others' needs is a more shadowy testament to our lack of ability to adapt and compromise. But like any language, adaptation and compromise can be learned. Today, for the future of the human species, we need to relearn these as soon as possible.

If you meet and are interested in someone from another cultural background, the ability to learn to adapt and compromise is even more valuable. Aside from the fact that *girls and guys are basically from different cultures*—each are socialized so differently that communication is often notoriously difficult—you can add a whole bunch of other differences quite rapidly. Another shadowy fact: about ninety-five percent of marriages in North America are within the same social class. Even religion is not as great a barrier to marriage as is class position. Rich people marry other rich people, poor other poor. In part this is due to a highly hierarchical society where we just don't come into contact with those better or worse off than ourselves. Our schools are arranged that way. If they are not done so publicly, the wealthy arrange schooling for their kids on their own. Private and charter schools abound. The rich don't want to mix with us regular folks. But we cannot be self-righteous about it. We in our turn don't want to mix with the poor. There *is* class warfare in Western democracies. It just comes out in an indirect way. People look to their social class peers for support and affirmation. They want to believe that they can make it. They want to know they are doing the right thing. None of us can be sure, if we are put into a different cultural setting, that what we know is worth anything at all. It is fair to say that there are many different realities in large-scale society. We do not cross the boundaries between them very much.

One way that some do is by going to university. If you are from a lower social class, the university was historically not for you. It is more open now. But this opening is deceptive. Once you're in, you will find that the language, the assumptions of the people who work there, and almost all your fellow students are middle class. It really is a different language. Not perhaps as different as that between male and female, but still noticeable. You'll have to study up on the ways of people who you were taught were your enemy, or at least not your friend. But lower-class persons do graduate from university and move up the social ladder. *Their* children will be middle class. These kids' grandparents will be at a distance from them. The grandparents will find them to be spoiled brats, at worst, and maybe at the same time be proud that their family has moved up in the world.

Many teenagers assume they will go to university. But dropout rates at the university are higher than at high school. So be careful. Unless you are willing to go over to the side of a traditional enemy group, you may have some trouble getting through it.

Like I said earlier about school in general, communicating cross-culturally does not have to mean that you join the other group for good. You don't have to go native, as some anthropologists have done over the years. These people were obviously uncomfortable with their culture of origin. And you might be too. But the class warfare that rages in our democracies is spurred on by forces that are publicly defended and promoted, telling lower-class people that they are no good. Non-whites sometimes feel this attack as well, depending on their origins. Sometimes women do as well. If they are not considered pretty, teen girls are pushed to the margins quite quickly. It's the old gender resocialization stuff rearing its ugly head again.

Guys better like football, and girls better be lean enough for the cheer squad. If not, you're either gay or ugly, respectively. Teenagers can easily question these idiotic stereotypes, but when you do, you have to pay a price. You may go through school being unpopular and shunned. You'll have to find dates among the other dorks.

There is a war going on in our schools as well. In a way, it prepares you not merely for competing against other adults later on. It also prepares you for the idea that life is *about* conflict and choosing sides. We talked earlier about how dark our schools are for promoting this kind of attitude. Once that attitude is in the back of your mind, it's all too easy to act on it when you grow up.

People commonly state quite straightforwardly that they think their children are more important than other people's children. If it is within a social group, the language is toned down to my kids are special, better behaved, smarter, prettier, and more talented than yours. But the language of self-interest and vanity becomes much more transparently racist or nationalist when the other, whoever they are, is afar. When we see that the stranger is clearly from a different culture, we don't hold back. Our kids are now superior in every way. They are also worth more in terms of their lives. We might mourn the loss of other people's kids during a war—far more than we mourn their adults, since we tend not to do this at all—but we always say, "better theirs than mine."

It is the idea that our children are more valuable than the children of others that underlies our ability to still make war. We know war is bad, often evil. It degrades us as human beings and brings out our worst potential. We can be trained to become killing machines and other monsters. But we think that we must protect our children because they are better, by nature, than some other kids.

But just because we love them more—they are our own, after all—doesn't mean we cannot, or should not, love children and protect them in general. A famous modern philosopher once said that, *"The love we have for our own children does not exempt us from loving the children of the world."* Absolutely correct. We cannot ethically shrug off our collective responsibility for other human beings just because they are not like us, or because they don't like us. In fact, we make enemies by doing so. If our political policies were different, if they were less self-interested, we would not have the conflicts we have in the world today. It is that simple. *Less selfishness, less conflict.*

We are aware as well that communication and conflict are related. The less of the one, the more of the other. We put a premium on representing ourselves in the best possible light. It is almost something sacred to us. When scientists sent Voyager One, a deep-space probe, into the void, they stuck on its side a golden recording of a great diversity of sounds from Earth, including all kinds of sounds, languages, singing, and poetry of human beings. We thought that in the remote chance that some aliens would encounter the craft, there would be a chance that they could understand some of what we are about. It is a noble idea, one that brings out the very best in us. A welcoming hand reaching out to the stars. It represents a grand human ideal.

But our reality on earth seldom lives up to that ideal. We need to try much harder to do so, because warfare in today's world carries an ultimate cost to it. This cost is completely different than the price of war before 1945. Our technology can now destroy all life on earth. Nothing left at all. Even the awesome and terrifying destruction of the Second World War pales in comparison. And just because nuclear war is out of the news and talking about it unfashionable, the threat remains, all the more so because we are currently not interested in the topic and therefore not paying attention to it.

As young people, you can't afford to assume that adults will take care of stuff for you. You need to also study up on the threats to your lives. War is one of them. Nuclear war is simply the last resort available to us to get what we want. Of course, in that case, no one gets anything at all. This is perhaps the chief reason why we have not had a nuclear war, at least not yet. We know what occurs. We have had two small samples, in Japan, at the very end of the second world war. In spite of the sacrifice involved, one would think that it would be important to have a real example of what happens when you drop atomic bombs on cities. No one would volunteer for such an experiment, so the sentiment is fraught with racism and nationalism. Even so, the deeds were done, and we know what it is like. This, too, has helped us. But sadly, we have not yet taken those terrible lessons to heart enough to get rid of our weapons. We keep them because we imagine they give us security and peace of mind. In fact, they give us the very opposite.

We can deny the anxiety their presence produces. We can claim that the threat they pose keeps our enemies from attacking us. But this attitude assumes that having enemies is forever. A motto that teens use often, 'friend forever,' has its opposite in this attitude. It is short-sighted, selfish, and promotes fear rather than understanding. Most teens in high school think that they will be friends forever. We know that doesn't always, or even often, occur. People change.

Our politics can as well. Politics are things people do. Since people can change, the politics can change with them. 'Enemies forever' just isn't the case. Russia's closest and most friendly ally in Europe is, of all places, Germany. My dad, a veteran of the Second World War, never could wrap his head around this. It can work when you don't even know the other well. Russia and India are close, though they have basically had nothing to do with each other historically. The United States and Britain is the most common example of this kind of change. They love each other now. But it was not at all always like that. When Canadian and British troops stormed Washington and burned the White House to the ground in 1814, things were quite different. The point is, we need to work for these kinds of changes. To be comfortable with *having* enemies is a paradox. It makes no sense in the long term.

The stakes are as high as they can be. Nuclear war is not an option. Yet we think that it is. If we didn't, there would be no nuclear weapons sitting around. Yes, we have made strides over the past generation to get rid of a lot of them. The amount of weapons trained on world cities has dropped significantly, with only a few hundred hard-alert warheads and launchers on each side today. In the 1980s, there were thousands. But these few hundred have the firepower to do damage from which the human species could not recover.

When I graduated from high school, way back in 1984, the university I was going to had a student union building. Inside, it was rumored that they had managed to get a stock of cyanide pills, which the student union promised would be given out to students in the event of a war. My generation, small as it is, grew up with the sense that the world was going to end at any moment. Imagine your high school graduation and prom with this in the back of your mind. No one wants to live like that. In fact, no one *can*. So on the one hand, we have reduced nuclear arsenals and other weapons of mass destruction. And we rather hypocritically try to limit their spread. The case of Iran is utmost in many minds today.

But would it not be better to lead by example? We could get rid of our nuclear weapons and *still* maintain a superior technology that would be able to prevent other rogue states from using theirs. But we have not done so. Yet there has been progress, even so.

On the other hand, the issue has gradually disappeared from the news. We have lost interest in it, or have pretended to. Teenagers today don't live with the anxiety of my generation when we were your age. That is a good thing. But consider how you have avoided living with it. The reality has not changed. You are in denial. Worrying about stuff doesn't help the cause, of course, but being in denial means that you think that there *is no cause* for worry. This is a fantasy. There is every cause for concern about the future of the human species. The clamor regarding the environment is one such concern. War is another. Plague might be a third. The risk of collision with an asteroid or comet might be a fourth. It has happened before. It killed off the dinosaurs, a group of species that dominated the earth for sixty-five million years. We like dinosaurs in our entertainment. Perhaps they remind us of ourselves.

Teenagers shouldn't be growing up in fear. But neither should they be growing up in ignorance. The two are intimately related. Ignorance breeds fear. Fear of the other cautions against experience. In this way, our fear lends weight to our ignorance. It is quite rational to fear war, especially all-out nuclear war. With ultimate war, we need not fear about an aftermath. There will not be many of us left. Those who are will not last long.

Speaking of entertainment, scary movies are often kind of fun. They provide a cheap thrill because we know that what occurs in them cannot be real. You want to see a real horror movie? Find and watch *The Day After*, a Hollywood film from 1983. It appeared at the end of the Cold War, when there were protests around the world regarding people's fear of nuclear holocaust. People were very aware at this point that we were living on the edge of the ultimate abyss. One word of advice: don't watch it alone.

We still live on that edge, but we have gotten used to it in an odd way. War is something that happens to other people. We see some of it in the media, though war reporting is highly censored. In fact, the Viet Nam War became a divisive issue for Americans in part because the television reporting of that era was not as censored. People saw the full horror of what their young sons were doing and suffering. They didn't like it. People don't want war. We put up with it because it remains at a distance.

There is an even greater hypocrisy at work in our society. In countries that do not have mandatory military service, only young people from marginal social groups 'volunteer' for the military. The vast majority of recruits are doing so because it is a paying job. It is a last resort for many. Hardly anybody is keen on joining up. Those who are, a modern professional military has no use for. They are unreliable in times of crisis and can't be trusted in combat. They take unnecessary risks, and thus put their comrades at risk. War mongers may exist, but the militaries of the world shun them.

The macho quality of being in the military is muted today. It's not about cartoon heroism. It's about having a job and a paycheck. It is about being unlucky. The numbers of privileged people who volunteer are few. Most go into officer training at famous places like West Point. They can be killed in combat too, of course. But their reasons for joining are either the same as their subalterns, or they are archaic. To get people to kill and die for you requires much specialized training. It is physical and psychological. It looks a little like brainwashing. It boils down to a set of skills you need to increase your survival quotient day to day in a time of crisis.

One of the key skills is one of most shadowy. It generates a percentage that is called a 'kill-ratio'. This percentage denotes the ability of however many soldiers to look down the gun-sights and pull the trigger, knowing that they are shooting to kill. Most people have a tough time doing this, even with military training. During the Second World War, allied kill ratios hovered around twenty-five percent. This means that about every one in four times you actually took aim and tried to kill your opponent. You stared him down in your sights and pulled the trigger. People fantasize about such a moment, rather perversely. But when it comes to actually doing it, it's not what we imagine. It's a key part of training ground troops that they be able to do this successfully as much as possible. But training back then wasn't up to the task. With one exception: The SS were the elite forces of the Nazis. As we mentioned before, they not only believed in what they were doing, they enjoyed it. *Their* kill ratios hovered around ninety percent. That's why they were so feared in combat. They had enormous odds against them for about half the war. They performed miracles of victory against vastly superior forces on both the Eastern and Western fronts. They slowed the pace of the ultimate allied victory significantly. Why? Because the Nazis had figured out how to train their recruits to *enjoy killing*. If you like something, if it gives you pleasure, you are much more likely to want to do it. The vast majority of soldiers on all sides never attained this dubious pitch of pleasure. How could any normal human being do that? Well, we can, if we are given the right set of circumstances. It is sobering to note that all nations after the war tried to adopt the SS techniques in the training of their own soldiers. In Viet Nam, kill ratios were gotten up to about fifty percent. Not too bad. About half the time you could rely on your comrades to shoot straight. In World War Two and before, many soldiers deliberately missed if they had a good target. Others just randomly busted off without even looking. Snipers were a hot commodity. They often attained higher rank and better pay for their rare skills.

Most of the skills soldiers and others learn are quite rational and handy to know. I wouldn't mind knowing more of them, though not at the price of joining up. I was a member of a paramilitary group myself, the Boy Scouts. This organization, so honored today, was founded in Britain by a fellow who would have been a Nazi had he not been born too early. The skills you learn in Scouting are handy, especially if you love being out in nature, as I do. But many of the ideas that are popular in these organizations are militaristic, bigoted, and sexist. It is modeled on the military. That's why I referred to it as 'paramilitary.' Some teenagers are members. They might be considered geeks by their peers, but this is no reason not to join. There are other, much better reasons for avoiding quasi-military youth organizations. Looking back on it, the experiences we had, other than camping and learning useful skills, makes me shudder.

And if it takes years of special training to become a willing killer and willing to put your life on the line for other people who are *not* willing to reciprocate, then it doesn't take as much to get people to join. For that, all we need to do is reproduce the social class hierarchy of our current society. "Let the lower class kids fight for us," the middle and wealthy class people say to themselves. Or if it is not said, which it seldom is, this is another example of denial. *That military service is not really voluntary* is another secret adults and politicians don't talk about.

Teens are dimly aware that something is odd when you talk about being able to die for your country but not able to drink a beer. But killing and dying for any cause, real or imagined, is much more serious than drinking beer. The two issues actually do not have that much to do with one another. The key thing is that through the fortune or misfortune of being born, something no one chooses to do, you might have to kill or die. Someone else will not have to.

This is the fundamental hypocrisy of having professional militaries without regular mandatory service or call-up in times of crisis. But if we had *that*, we would have to face the consequences of thinking that war is an option. I can guarantee you that if middle-class parents saw their kids go off to their potential deaths, there would be a lot *less* support for the wars we still fight. All of a sudden war would be a harsh reality for too many. Instead of being able to be in denial and shrug off the fact that lower-class parents have to face this reality on their own, we would have to own up to it ourselves. All the good kids in school would be carrying guns and looking grim. Goodness into badness at the drop of a helmet. All the pretty girls, the cute guys, the popular kids, the honor roll. All conscripted and turned into something not as nice, not as warm. *That's* what's fair in a society that prepares for war on the cheap.

No one would really want this. But this just points up the hypocrisy. *Do lower-class parents feel less love for their kids? Do their kids feel less pain than ours?* In tough economic times, like right now, we do see more of the lower- and middle-class kids having to join up. We get a little taste of what justice is in relation to a fundamentally unjust social and political expectation. Human blood is just that. It runs within us all. It runs from us when we are injured. It drains our life away if we cannot heal ourselves. The lifeblood of our communities rests in our children. Do we really want to see them living as if they were some other species, some other and better kind of human being? Do we want them to grow up thinking that they are responsible only to themselves? That other people's children exist to serve them? I would go so far to say that those kinds of attitudes are evil. They lead to disasters like the Holocaust. They allow us to live at the expense of others.

Because there are rare times when we have an enemy who would rather kill and die than anything else, who is fanatical and therefore has taken their humanity to a level where we have to defend ourselves, war cannot get a zero rating. We may need to defend ourselves. The Taliban seem to be such a group. It is also prudent to maintain purely defensive weapons, like anti-ballistic missiles and fighter interceptors and tactical submarines, just in case something goes wrong in some other country. But these are the exceptions. Otherwise, war is evil. It causes human suffering on a grand scale. It is a testament to our failure to do the work necessary to understand and cooperate with one another. *We must all do this work on a daily basis.* Teenagers can start at home with the parents that they sometimes go to war with. Adults can start with their children, reassuring them that they are not their enemies. Not forgetting that we sometimes may fail, I will rate war a one out of ten.

9. The Secrets of Religion (and belief)

~~~~~~

You cannot live without faith. It is a delusion to think that one is faithless. It is degrading to attempt it. But having faith can mean believing in something other than an established religion. Faith is a necessity for human existence. This is so because we cannot know the future. This future is our own, but we cannot own it. And the ultimate future of all life is death. Knowing this does not prevent faith. It justifies it in the strongest possible terms. But belief, faith, and religion are often confused. People think that they are the same thing or that you have to have all three to have any. Yes, beliefs do require faith on our part, in that they are unlike some kinds of experiences where we think we know what is going on and there is no room for belief. But this difference is about how we think about them. All forms of human knowledge require a kind of faith. This is because humans cannot know things beyond their experience.

We experience things every day. They are mostly trivial and commonplace. We expect the expected. We even get used to it enough to like it. It is comforting to just do your thing without surprises. We simply want to get on with our lives. We don't need unusual distractions. This is likely why, when things get too dull, we contrive distractions out of second lives in the world of cyberspace, or we go to a scary film. We know it isn't real. When we're done, we can return to our regular lives and get on with it.

But what, exactly, are we getting on with? Having real experiences means being taken out of the regular flow of life. An authentic experience is one that shatters our preconceptions about things—what we thought we knew we in fact didn't. This is why we can talk about all experiences having a negative quality to them. This does not mean that they are bad. It means, more narrowly that they *negate* our previous experience in a sudden way.

This negation of what we thought we knew means that a real experience has happened to us. It occurs without our planning for it. In a sense, experience happens without our consent. Such experiences as these make us doubt what we took for granted. It could be anything. Your friends might betray you or they might declare their love for you. Marriages fall apart because people change. You could even ace a course you hated. You could find out something about your parents that you really didn't want to know. The negative quality of real experience takes us by surprise. It does not let us get away with thinking that we know all about this or that.

There is always something new just over the horizon of where we have been and what we have seen. Young people often go on treks to different parts of the world after high school or university. They want to get out and see what's there. You know you have grown up with only one kind of thing, the world immediately around you. For a while, this is very comforting. But suddenly you want to break out of it, even change the way you live, see how other people get along and what they think about things. These experiences are calculated in the sense that you put yourself out there. But what happens to you during such a process is often beyond your control. Yet you are open to it.

Both the sudden and unexpected quality of real experience and the seeking of these kinds of experiences used to be associated with religion. Someone had a vision, say, and interpreted it in a certain way. Or someone strikes out from their community in search of truth. New religions are said to have started in these ways. And indeed, when you do have new experiences, it does give you a sense that there is another world out there. This new world is one that you knew nothing about before. It can have an earth-shattering effect.

In previous ages of humankind, the shattering of previous prejudice was so impressive that people interpreted it as having come from another world: the world of the gods, or from God himself. Only God could change your mind. This was thought because human experience was more local than it is today. Contact with other cultures and the sheer knowledge of what is going on around the world has increased exponentially over the past century. You can get news from anywhere. You can look up anything on the Internet. We are less liable to be impressed by something other than ourselves.

In this way, it is more difficult for us today to have really shattering experiences. For better or worse, the ones we do have *do* tend to be negative in the regular sense. Someone close to you dies, for example. The world is forever changed. But it is not the case that our ancestors were more parochial than us. They lived in cultures where the gods might break into ordinary experience at any time. They were, in this sense, prepared for the unexpected and the unusual in a way that we are not. In this way, it is we who are more provincial in our thinking than them. We know more. They experienced more. Because of this difference, interpretation of what has happened to you takes a different tack.

We tend not to interpret strange experiences in a religious way. They did. But just because we don't jump to the conclusion that God is speaking to us doesn't mean that our search for meaning is any different than theirs was. This is so because striking out from your comfort zone, your society, and friends and family, means taking a leap of faith. Similarly, when you do experience the unexpected and it moves you to get rid of what you thought you knew, the new knowledge that is so strange to you also requires of you a leap of faith. On the one hand, faith supports our effort to try something new in the simplest manner. Anything we have not done before, especially as children, might seem difficult and unimaginable. But it is adults who really need faith in this way. Young people, especially teenagers, are eager— sometimes overeager—to try out the new. Many of you are either in your first years of university or will be shortly going there. You know, for example, how to study, how to take exams, how to get to class on time, how to sit and listen to a lecture. This is all boring stuff you have done so many times before. It is a wonder any of you *do* darken the doors of your local college.

But when you look around your new classroom at the university it is not the same. The first thing you will notice is the presence of older adults. These people would not even be allowed on high school grounds, let alone in the classroom. What are they doing there? They are students, just like you are. Some will be as old as your parents, some even older. Folks who have retired, for instance, and have gone back to school. They now have, for whatever reason, an opportunity to do something that they never did before. Very often it is retirement, change of or loss of job, or divorce that gets older people back into the classroom.

Whatever the reason, they all have one thing common: guts. Plain and simple, non-traditional students, as they are called, have a basic courage that they can actually do something they either have never done or have not done in years. And their courage is founded on one thing alone—faith. Some of them have fun being with you. Their own kids have moved out and they miss them. But just as often I see them rolling their eyes in pain or disbelief at your naivety about the world. They actually have been there, done that. You have not. They are not trying to dismiss you. Your experiences, coming from a new generation, will in fact be different from theirs.

They often forget that while they have been doing other things, the world has changed. The world waits for none of us. It goes on its way, and we are the ones who must adapt. But all adaptation calls for new experiences. You see these older students and you might think, *I am glad I am not them.* You might imagine that they are getting a really late start on life. But you'd be wrong. Their lives started decades ago. They've just been running on different paths. It is the mixture of these different paths and experiences that makes for a great learning experience in the classroom and outside of it. The best thing you can do as teenagers right now is contact older people, even your grandparents, and ask them how they think the world has changed and why.

Doing this will help you get a sense that the world is much wider and more diverse than you imagined. People you thought you knew well will tell you things you didn't dream of, stuff they experienced or did that you would not suspect of them. Just because they're old doesn't mean that they haven't lived. And people can pack a lot of living into a few years. The sense that we only have so long to live is something that teenagers don't really understand. It is well known that teens don't expect or really know that they can die. This understanding comes about in various ways, but commonly only around age twenty-one or twenty-two. It is a key feature in maturing. The knowledge of one's own limited lifespan changes everything. Today, it is the source of much anxiety, more than in the past. Why? Because we live in an age that has begun to see the abandonment of traditional religions and the kinds of faith associated with them.

We are no longer believers. We do not trust our governments. We do not trust authority. In fact, a good part of this book has cautioned you against such a trust. Blind belief has little merit. But to say that our ancestors were blind because they were more religious than us is unfair. In fact, they felt strongly that they *knew* the truth of things. God or the gods *had* spoken to them or someone they knew. The priests or priestesses *were* in touch with the other world. They had one foot in it and one foot in our own. They translated the messages from the gods into a language we could understand. People believed because they felt they had experience of this other reality. This strange reality was on a higher plane than our own. It was the source of our reality, for the gods had created the world and us in it. Every religion of the period of agriculture said the same thing about creation. Timelines varied, from moments to six days to billions of years. But the result was the same. The world of humans was linked in the most intimate fashion with the world of spirits.

But today the world of spirits is seen as a myth. Only our world remains, cut off from any other. This change has come about in a complex way. The rise of scientific explanation has eroded the territory of religious explanation. But this alone cannot explain the shift in thinking. As well, most people around the world still believe in a God of some kind. It is about ninety percent. Even so, these beliefs have increasingly become personalized. That is, one keeps such beliefs inside oneself, private. This changes religion and faith. They become more about what you can do and what you are willing to believe than about meanings that are widely shared.

We live on in a kind of blindness that we can know the truth of things by ourselves. This is not to say that each of us must in fact find such a truth to live on our own. It is no good living by someone else's truth. A great religious philosopher from India famously stated that "Truth is a pathless land." Each of us, whether from the East or West, appears to be on our own path, making it up as we go along.

This is one way to cope with the loss of a shared and smaller-scale culture. We tend to live in giant and diverse countries. Most of us claim this or that religion, but when you look deeper, the oneness of any religion fractures along many different lines. Sects, even cults, arise all around us. Religions as well as churches with the same name can be very different once you step inside them. So what is going on here? Why is there a first Baptist church, and then down the road, a second Baptist church, and so on? If your friends go to church at all, why isn't it the same one your family goes to? Why do some Catholics pay attention to the pope while others do not? Why do people who claim a different religion seem to hate us? I already suggested that religion is only a rationalization for conflict, not a true source. Certainly when you look at religions that began in a specific historical period, no matter what region they are from, they are all basically saying the same thing. The way in which it is said may differ. But this difference is one of culture, not belief. The history of the start of religions exposes their messages. To think that because religion or a specific church has a history means that what it says is a fraud is misguided. Religions are for human beings. They function in an important way for us even today. If they did not, there would be little interest in them. The spirits and gods in whom people believe do not need religion. They are the sources of religious faith. They are said to know the truth and not seek it, as we do.

Because most human beings have an interest in seeking truth, we have looked to religions to help us out. Faiths are literally supposed to guide us toward the light. To believe is to have faith that what you're doing is the right way or the right thing. Of course, this can be dangerous. People can be blinded by the light as well. They no longer can see what others see. They have lost all human perspective. But there is a balance between seeking superhuman truth and remaining true to one's human roots. Let's take a look at the basic types of truth-seeking. There are, surprisingly, very few of them. All other religious variations come out of, or react to, the following five types:

a) There is no true God; all Gods are false.
b) There is one true God, but God takes many forms and all forms are true.
c) There are many different Gods, and all are true.
d) There are many different Gods but only some are true
e) There are many Gods, but only one is true.

All five patterns may be seen historically. In fact, the earliest known religions that we are aware of were not really interested in the idea of God at all. At most, small-scale hunting and gathering peoples tend to say, if asked, "Oh yeah, God created the world a long time ago, and we have not heard anything from him since then." There are religions without gods, so we should not immediately think that category 'a' means only atheism. But we should pay specific attention to atheism within category 'a' because it is the most likely alternative for you as teenagers if you feel distrustful toward religion.

Don't be fooled. *Atheism is a religion.* It just happens to be the religion of no god. In this it comes across as a most nonsensical belief. Atheism borrows all of the character of religion but inverts the goal of religion. The goal of revealed religion is to know God. 'Revealed' just means someone has had a vision, or there has been a message from on high, like with Moses or Muhammad, or someone has discovered hidden scriptures. Of course people have faith that there is a God. That is the whole point. But atheists have the exact same kind of faith, that there is *no* God. In this they are as delusional as they claim traditional believers are. They are not at all free of religion. If you become an atheist, aside from unfair stigmata, you might get from friends and family and certain schools, you will have to face up to the fact that you have merely traded one belief for another. From the atheist's claimed perspective, their beliefs would be just as false! That is, if an atheist is an atheist because he thinks that people who have faith are stupid, he must include his own faith in that same category. More than this, and from an atheistic perspective mind you, the atheist does come across as even more stupid than us regular religious folks. This is because the atheist *denies* that he has a faith when in fact he does have one. No other religion denies that it is a religion!

So I cannot recommend atheism. It is blind about the character of its own faith. Just because it does not have a god does not mean it is every bit as religious, and hence potentially delusional, as every other religion. Atheism is *not* an option for those who want to free themselves of religious belief. Instead, you have to turn to agnosticism. But first, we need to clarify this position. This is a bit of a misnomer. The name, in other words, does not quite fit the bill. Mystics have existed all through religious history. One of their basic things was that you could not really come to know the character of God, even though 'gnosis' itself refers to 'knowledge.' They would simply say that "All I think of God, *that*

God is not." 'That' meaning what they thought of God, of course. They defined God by negation. God was so different from humanity—this makes sense, after all—that humans could not really know what God was or what he was about. So 'gnosticism' has this mystical quality about it. So 'agnosticism' should strictly mean the fullest opposite of this, even though the word does negate 'knowledge.' In the same way, a 'theist' is a believer, and an 'atheist' is an unbeliever. But then agnosticism would mean what most other kinds of religions already say! If gnosticism or a mystical variant thereof denies we can know God without some kind of extra-human help, then agnosticism or its variants would claim that we *can* know God. Or, if you take it strictly on the term itself, that we cannot have knowledge (of Gods or whatever). This is clearly *not* what agnosticism means today. It refers to a position of open-minded skepticism. It is the correct 'belief' for a scientist to hold, for example. The agnostic is someone who neither believes that there is a God nor believes that there is no God. It's a kind of wait-and-see attitude. It is befitting of our modern disposition to be skeptical, even distrustful of authority and tradition. The 'a' at the front of the term suggests a *lack* of knowledge. The key thing here is that agnosticism is *not* religious.

It actually does what atheism claims for itself. The agnostic is free of religious belief. But they are open to returning to it if events warrant. The agnostic is less prone to delusion and dogmatism than some religious people. It is a healthy position for those who do not want to take on the religion of their parents. Even better, it is a good position for those who are waiting patiently to understand how life works. You can, in other words, move from agnosticism to this or that religious belief if you experience something that changes your life and makes you feel the desire to believe in another world or in a God. This is what occurred to me, for instance. The details are many and not important here. But it showed that the way I felt about religion or metaphysical beliefs in general was not narrow or close-minded. It was open to the very kinds of experiences that make us human and guide us toward the humane.

So I *can* recommend agnosticism. Agnosticism provides a space where you can think things out on your own. You may have to wait until your own death to learn what you need to know. So be it. Nothing wrong with that. The mistake is to close yourself off to new experiences, whatever their source and however you want to interpret them. That is what atheism and many other religions do. But if you already are part of a religion, you may have already had the experiences you need to get where you're going, so no worries.

So much for category 'a' above. What about the others? Category 'b' is also a very common take on these things, though a recent one. When confronted by the bewildering diversity of human religious beliefs around the world, it is understandable that someone would simply say, "Well, all are true." It's an easy position to hold. You keep the idea of there being one true God, but because of God's powers and love for all humans, he shows himself in whatever form these or those humans need from him. No problem. Except there is a problem. The other religions that you have just supplied their source for don't agree with you. Some of them do not think there is but one God with many forms. Some think there are many Gods or that God does not show himself to other believers, only us. So if you are into category 'b,' and many are, you need to be aware that it allows *you* comfort and has nothing to do with the reality of religious diversity.

The 'one God many forms' idea is on the surface culturally tolerant. But underneath the surface it is culturally imperialist. This means that you have smuggled in your own beliefs about God and religion and hidden them beneath the beliefs of others. You have imported your own beliefs and stacked them onto others. You may be able to convince these others that there is actually only one God but that he has infinite variety and character. But the point is, in doing so you will have gotten them to depart from *their* traditional beliefs. This in itself is not a bad thing. But it should be recognized for what it is. You are, in your own hippiesque and apparently tolerant way, no different from a missionary.

In fact, many people in North America praise themselves without good reason for their tolerance. We see how people suffer in other countries and cultures and thank God that we are not like them. We are more mature. We have grown up to the point of saying, "Let's all get along with one another." But in fact our version of live and let live allows us to live the way we want while the others can go to hell. We have already seen some of this in reference to politics and war. Religion, when it is dishonest with itself, can function in the same way. It allows us to carry on as we were without being the least bit challenged by the beliefs and realities of other people. Atheism does this and claims it doesn't. Dogmatic religions do it and think they are right. And so does category 'b,' though more gently and thus, ironically, less honestly. But the thing they all share is the ability to be oblivious to real differences. They want to flatten everything out into their own thing. This is not the way of authentic religious or spiritual faith. It owns up to its own beliefs and admits that others may be right and it wrong.

Which brings us to category 'c.' Here, instead of smuggling our idea of God into other religions, we simply say that all religions are true by their own definitions. The key then becomes *who* believes, and not *what* they believe. If you believe in this or that, then it is true for you. Category 'c' is a kind of relativism. This just means that you really do live and let live. You're beliefs are not more right and true than the next person's. And you're willing to go with that. You can respect the beliefs of others while not believing in them. To a point, at least.

Mostly, we avoid each other on those topics, which is why teenagers are told by their parents that when company is over, there is to be no talking about politics and religion. As if teens would talk about these subjects anyway! Category 'c' makes sense anthropologically, sociologically, and psychologically. There is a time-honored saying in social science that runs, "If people believe something to be real, it is real in its consequences." This suggests that whatever the source of belief, revealed or otherwise, that is not important. What are important are the *consequences* of holding a particular belief. And every belief has its own set of consequences.

Consider the difference between believing that you are immortal versus not. Aside from the delusion in life that you can do anything and not risk life and limb, the entire idea of the world and its place in the cosmos changes. With one, there is an afterlife. It does not matter, as we shall see later, what kind it is. The fact is that you go on. That what *this* is, is not *all* there is. The opposite of that is true for the person who believes only in mortality. Big difference! The consequences of how you act and what you live for are very different depending on what you believe in. And those consequences in terms of your actions and goals *are* real. They are real in a way that the sources of your beliefs are not, or do not need to be. This idea, original to American philosophy, tells us that you have to rely on the fruits of belief and not its roots. If religion, for example, does not do anything good for a society, than abandon it. No matter where it claims to be from, even from a God himself. Get rid of it if it no longer works. But if a religion that has some other source does work, then keep it. Now almost all religions claim a higher source, so discriminating among them on those grounds is unnecessary. But the point remains. *Belief is not false if it truly works in your life.* Belief is only a fraud when you are taken in by it and it harms you. So the idea of delusion, or a fixed false belief, can only be judged by whether or not the fruits of the belief make your life better or not. If the consequences of you holding this or that belief make your life worse and you continue to hold onto it, you are delusional.

But you cannot always be objective about this kind of judgment. With things like drugs, I think you can. But with religion, not at all. Atheists would like to think that they are objective in their condemnation of all religion. We have already seen how hollow and hypocritical that claim is. But for some, no doubt, religion is after all a bad thing. It leads them into serious mistakes. It might make them sacrifice their lives for an evil cause. It might make them harm others in the name of God. All this cannot be denied, even if it seems we are apologizing for religious belief in this chapter.

But equally so, religion can inspire us to the best we can be. It can create real communities of people who care about one another without harming those not like them. It can set a goal for the species as a whole to come together as humanity, which is our collective birthright. The history of religion is not solely a history of fraud and delusion. So category 'c' is a starting point. If you take it to mean that religious beliefs are real because the consequences for those who believe in them are real, then this is solid. You don't have to become a theologian to make this point. You *do* have to, however, be honest about your beliefs and realize that because the world does not share them, it means either you or they or both of you are wrong in some way.

What of the last two categories? These two I consider to be highly unlikely in terms of their claim to be the way things are, given the nature of belief in general. Category 'd' says that though there are many Gods, only some of them are true. There is no way to state that some cultures have gotten things right and others wrong. There is good and evil in every society. Everyone makes mistakes. Perhaps a combination of all of our wisdom is the real truth, at least for humans. But the idea that certain cultures have a hold on truth and others none at all is nonsense. This is what category 'd' implies, and not just about religion or belief in God. It can be dismissed precisely because of this implication.

Category 'e' implies something even worse. God has shown himself in his true form to only one culture or set of ideas. Everyone else is left behind, as it were. This is not only nonsense but gives rise to the worst kind of thinking and action imaginable. The unenlightened are now less than human, or merely human. The twice-born are in the know and will ascend to heaven. The rest of us will not. This kind of thinking is not at all limited to certain forms of Christianity. All large-scale religions have their groups who think like this. The Taliban are an easy example. And they are a good one, too. Because once you start to think like this, anything becomes possible. The beliefs are realized in their consequences. And the consequence for the rest of us is torture and death.

So, these folks say you should join us! Eventually the whole world will think like us and there will be no problem. When I lived in Mississippi, I once saw a bumper sticker that said, "One World, One God, Jesus." It reminded me immediately of the Nazi slogan "One People, One Blood, One Leader." Now I didn't know if the vehicle owner was a category 'b' believer, but I suspect that he was in category 'e.' It's a terrible risk to think like this. But it also might only be an advertisement of a faith that hopes and has a name. The *name* matters not, the *hope* is in fact important.

One could go to a Muslim country and perhaps read the same sticker, if they do bumper stickers at all, except Jesus would be replaced with another name. No real problem here, if *that* was what the driver believed. But I doubt it. It is category 'e' that turns many people off from religion. Teenagers especially feel this because you are told in no uncertain terms what you should and should not believe about things. Schools, families, churches, and governments all force-feed you their beliefs. To reject them is also dangerous. But you need to maintain a healthy distance from all of these institutional and official forms of belief. No one who has ever started a new religion has obeyed the going authority, including Jesus.

In a way, none of these categories is very inspiring. The first simply denies the importance of religion. The second smuggles in your own religion at the expense of someone else's. The third works, but it can only take you so far. The last two have no merit and are based in cultural prejudices. So where do we go from here? Category 'c' is the safest and most ethical bet, but you have to work on it yourself to make it sincere. First of all, ignore what other people believe. This sounds odd. What I mean is, don't let what other folks say necessarily be your truth. Let things play themselves out. This may take years. You might need to develop a kind of agnosticism. This may not extend all the way to an idea of God, but it would include the beliefs of those around you. Maybe they're right. Maybe they're not. Maybe they are right sometimes and other times wrong. This is, in fact, very much like reality. Staying real does not mean buying into official propaganda about anything. It means looking at the world as it is, with all its errors and mistakes, and with all kinds of different people believing in different things. You should never abandon this part of your wait-and-see attitude.

But in the meantime, you are going to have experiences, sometimes of the sort I started out this chapter talking about, stuff that will blow your mind, stuff that you thought could never happen to you, or even someone like you. It can happen. It does happen. Some of you will want to interpret these experiences in a religious way, some will not. Your interpretations will depend on your past experience. In this way, the 'shattering of prior prejudice' has to be understood by taking what you thought you knew about the world and reconstructing it. It won't come back to you the same. It is not a reboot. We are not machines. No, we are as human as the next person, and this means our neighbors or the almost unrecognizable person from the farthest corner of the earth. Each of us has the same task in this sense—to find meaning in a world that is made meaningful only by human beings and human history. Religion has been a major way of doing this, perhaps *the* major way. To abandon it now just because some people think it is old fashioned or delusional is to in fact participate in a delusion.

This is going to sound oddly conservative and old fashioned, but I want to suggest that even if you don't believe in God, think about joining a church or religious community in your area. You will have to be cautious. There are two kinds of churches out there, and I am not talking about the right and wrong ones according to some abstract truth. No, I mean the churches where people go to see and be seen. These are the false churches, no matter what beliefs they claim to espouse. People attend them to network with each other for ulterior proposes, like business deals, marriage opportunities, and local political schemes. The real churches are those where, when you go, you feel a sincere and caring community of others. These people will over time become part of your life and you will be able to rely on them and trust them to help you in a compassionate manner. In spite of all the abuses some churches perpetrate and try to hide, in spite of all the suffering that fanatics have led us to throughout history, *no* other institution, as yet, has been able to provide the kind of community we humans actually need in our lives. Not workplaces, not governments, not universities, not community groups who have a cause. Perhaps benevolent associations have tried, but there again, the major reason these have existed is for people to network for ulterior motives, usually having to with business or local politics.

The funny thing about both these types of churches is that the sermons don't matter. No one is listening, either way. So if you are into networking and self-interest, consider a false church and don't be scared off by what you are hearing from the pulpit. Every study that has ever been done regarding church attendance has evidenced that people have not listened to the sermon. They cannot tell you what it was about, even stepping out the church door at noon.

People go to church to make community, either a false one or a true one. This is yet another thing atheists and other critics mistake about religion. Anyway, you can get what you want from a church organization whether you are sincere or just a jerk. If you are the former, see if you can find a church, or the equivalent depending on the sect, where compassion and community are the order of the day. Again, don't be scared off by the sermon's content. It's just words and ritual and it is expected. It is the communication that occurs among members, the intimate counsel of their pastor, and the presence of family, with all of its weaknesses and strengths, that make a good church deserve its reputation. If you get interested in going, or if you think you now need to change the one you're going to, you might try to start small. But not too small! Once in a while people get really weird and start up what might be legitimately called a cult.

Social scientists use this word to refer to any small religious group that has just started up. *All* churches were once cults, in this sense. But we are more used to hearing the casual meaning. It is always negative. In our scheme, a cult in this general sense would refer to category 'e' extremists. They have abandoned the sense that a wider group could share their beliefs. Only these very few people are in the truth and light. Contemporary cults usually end up in disaster. They are places of abuse, torture, brainwashing, and slavery. But the scientific sense of the word cult should not be ignored. It is in this sense that authentic religions also get their start—a few people, scattered over a region, coming together for shared needs and desires.

You might not know the historical secret that the original Christian cults, competing as they did with other Greek and Roman cults and those of the Near East, were one of the only ones to welcome both men and women together. It was literally come as you are. This proved to be a huge advantage in terms of marketing. The early Christians also engaged in sexual behaviors that are now certainly taboo, and part of the meaning of the Greek word 'agape' is in fact erotic. Who wouldn't want to join?

Don't expect wild orgies when you are welcomed as a newcomer to a modern church. But what you can hope to expect is *compassion*, which rates better than passion any day of the week. Religion is not entirely a good thing for human beings. The history of religion is drenched in bloodshed. Those who tried to be religious were either killed or gave into the killing and participated in it. Religion is often a home for the dogmatist, and religion allows you to be too comfortable with your own beliefs. But because religion can create authentic community, can make us aspire to better ourselves and help others without regard for self-interest, and because religious ideas about the cosmos have inspired our modern sciences, religion has much good in it as well. As such, I am going to rate it an equivocal five out of ten.

10. The Secrets of Death (and life)

〰〰〰〰〰〰〰〰〰〰〰〰〰〰〰〰〰〰〰〰〰〰

We're almost done. If you have read this far, I thank you. No doubt you have seen some things that have made you raise your eyebrows a little. You wanted to know what's what, after all. But now we arrive at the end. The final chapter: death itself. But there is no need to be melodramatic about it. A famous modern philosopher simply stated that "All those who live must accept death." He called us 'border crossers,' passing from this world to the beyond. But what is the beyond about? To respond to this, we actually have to turn back to our own world. For all visions of the afterlife are a response to what we see in the here and now.

Teenagers and younger children are blissfully unaware of their own mortality. That's the main reason why you guys take so many unnecessary risks. Why you're always so willing to try out new things no matter the danger. It's also about peer pressure, of course. Everyone is jumping off cliffs today, so I need to get over there and do it too. That sort of thing. Of course, and equally lame, adults always seem to think that whatever you're up to it must be bad, or at least mischievous.

Both teens and adults avoid thinking about death. As teens, you are still in that phase where life and the experience of living give no probable cause to suspect that there is anything else. Adults know about death but suppress this knowledge. No parent wants to hear of their child's death. It is one of the most critical blows a person can endure. It changes the survivors' lives forever. You never truly get over such a thing. But there are lots of lesser deaths that occur in

143

life. Indeed, they must occur if we are to grow beyond the present version of ourselves.

We kill ourselves off, figuratively, by committing a series of social suicides over the life course. Teens don't act like little kids, and you know that you resent it greatly when adults try to treat you like you still are. Young adults are not like those of middle age nor the elderly. There are lots of phases of human existence, that is, if you are lucky enough to experience all of them. The life expectancy in the African country of Botswana is thirty-six years, for instance. This means that if you had been born there, you have an average chance of living only that long. About half die younger, in other words. This type of average has not been seen in Western countries since the eighteenth century.

The fact that people live a long time in developed countries also gives us the sense that our deaths are something we can forget about. Adults try to think like teenagers about death by using statistics such as these. But we can't really pull it off. Something has happened to us, usually in our early twenties, that has changed our sense of who we are. Even more, it has changed our sense of *what* we are, and what we are to become. And what we are is mortal.

We know, seemingly suddenly, that we can die and we will die. We don't know when, of course. I mentioned earlier the Greek demigod Prometheus in connection with stealing fire from the gods. He also performed a much more important service on behalf of humans. *He hid from us the hour of own deaths.* All human projects, all of our hopes, dreams, ambitions, and visions, hinge on this. We know we will die, but we don't know when. Thus everything, in the meanwhile, becomes possible for us. It was the greatest service a god could perform. It is part of the essence of humanity.

So adults cannot predict when we will die, obviously. It is not about *that* kind of knowledge. But we do have an utterly different sense about what it is to live. We know now that *we live on in the face of death.* To be able to put aside this knowing and get on with life is a major mark of a mature human being. Teenagers don't need to do this. It may be cultural, it may be evolutionary, or it may have something to do with physiological growth. But young people who are still physically growing do not think about life as limited. Your lives seem to stretch out in front of you in an endless fashion. The days run into each other. It's like a long summer vacation. And then, you turn around, and you've graduated high school and you have to get on with your lives.

This is what adolescence looks like from an adult's perspective. Time zips by. But from what I can recall from my own time as a teen, it did not seem like this at all. All those grades. You finish one and two months later you start another, and then another. *That* is what seemed endless. But even that contributed to my sense that my life was also endless. Things just kept going, no matter what my friends and I got up to. But somewhere around twenty-one, I started to feel my own mortality for the first time. There was no sudden crisis. People I knew didn't start dropping dead all around me. What is it, then? I think it generally has to do with being placed in contexts where you encounter all ages and stages of life. I think the understanding of our own mortality is a gradual thing that happens when you are placed in diverse social settings. You see people aging. You see them without the ability to perform as they once did. You, who are at the top of your physical game, a twenty-something, buff and beautiful, are surrounded by the rest of us, who are neither. You begin to realize that the physical part of you will not always be this perfect. You learn to enjoy it while you still can. This kind of understanding takes time.

It begins with a somehow sudden sense that you too *can* die. It starts with 'can' well before the knowledge of 'will' appears. Persons a little older than you tend to say, "Yeah, I know I can die, but I won't." That lingers for a while until the fuller understanding takes over that one not only *can*, but *could*, and ultimately *will*. That fuller sensibility occurs somewhere around the mid-thirties in our society.

Here's a shameful story about myself: When I was thirty-two, I lost what I thought was my soul mate. She didn't die, of course. But her leaving was like a death to me. Nothing against her. I certainly wasn't the person I am today back then. Some seven months afterward, two days before my next birthday, I elected to drive in a raging blizzard through mountain roads back to my home. I was working in another town some five hours distant. I thought I would meet some friends and family and celebrate. I seemed to be blithely unaware of the risks. I was driving far too fast. I lost control of the car and it spun round and round on the slick surface. My life hung in the balance. But the car veered into the verge rather than into oncoming traffic, rolled completely over, and made a gentle landing in a large snowbank. I opened my eyes to find myself hanging upside down, seatbelt still on, car stereo still on. I managed to extricate myself from the crushed vehicle without a scratch. The guy who had been following me had of course stopped and had gotten out to assist. I stood up to see his face. His jaw was hanging on the ground, as it were. It took a few hours, but I had the sense that I had dodged a big bullet there.

But it took months before I began to think that what had happened was due to my depression and sense of loss from my relationship. I didn't really care about my life. This was the knowledge that I had to face. It took me six more years to fully comprehend the implications of that attitude. In the meantime, I continued to put myself at lesser risk, always having to do with the women I was subsequently with.

Even telling you this story here makes me ashamed. What the hell was I thinking? The fact was, I didn't need to think. I had accepted my own death in a passive way and therefore did not even try to avoid situations where I could be killed. The idea that my life was worthless just because some other person left me was, of course, shamelessly stupid. But this feeling is commonplace. Maybe I took the loss harder than some would. But even so, you'd think that someone that age would not take it so much to heart. When I look at myself now, with all my accomplishments, my attitude of that earlier time makes me wince. What a waste it would have been to die then!

The point of such a tale is to let you know that adults too sometimes take a long time to realize that this too shall pass. We, as well as teens, have that lingering sense that who we are and especially how we feel at the moment is how we are *always* going to feel, that we will *never* get over what has happened to us, that the rest of our lives will be stuck in the present day.

All of this is nonsense. But some of us have to get really lucky to learn that important lesson. I didn't have good adult counsel when I was a teenager. That is, in part, one of the reasons I wrote this book. The final chapter is a good place to let out that little secret. Yet I still managed to learn the necessary things to take care of myself. It came at a bigger cost than for some. But I never paid any grievous or ultimate price for my tardiness. The key for my wife and I, given our shared experiences, is to not be too overprotective of our daughter when she comes along. Kids and teenagers *need* to be unaware of their own deaths. This may seem odd, but the purpose of ending such a book with such a topic is to try to get you not to mature prematurely.

There's a classic American short story where a guy falls asleep on a sailing ship in one of those bunks where your nose is basically touching the board above you. He dreams, because of this cramped position, that he is actually in a wooden coffin and has been buried prematurely. He goes through all of these horrors until he wakes up and realizes where he really is. I was that guy. I had prematurely buried myself. I began to live the horror and shadows of death before I died.

This is the other part of how people can waste their lives away. They stop living. Usually we do this in response to some crisis, greater or lesser, great, as in the case of a real death of a lover or spouse who still did actually love us and want to be with us. Much less in the case I experienced. But we restart our sense of what it means to get on with our lives over the course of time. Human beings are amazingly adaptable on this point. It is part of the miracle of being human. We have to be this adaptable because all of us are mortal.

We react in typical fashion to the death of another. There are good deaths and bad deaths. Everyone in the same society knows what they are. The good death is simply afforded to someone we think has lived a fulfilling life, usually over a certain number of years. Children and teenagers cannot have good deaths. They were never given a chance to be fulfilled. But even middle-aged people, if they have done a lot of what they wanted to do, if they have made some big contribution to the wider community, can be said to have had a good death. Usually it has to be related to an illness that one could not control. A car accident is not a good death, for instance.

Where one dies is also part of the equation. Dying at home is seen as the best. The hospital or nursing home very much second best. In one's car or on one's bike, not good at all. But if you are a much older person, still healthy enough to be cycling, or if you loved to drive and collected sports cars, even these lesser places can take on the mantle of a good death. Bad deaths are always associated with either unnecessary happenings or youth or lack of life fulfillment. Being an innocent bystander at a crime scene is one example. Children who die in wars is another, or if you had just begun to really live and love for the first time and all of a sudden you got cut off. These sorts of deaths are almost always considered bad, even evil.

The worst deaths for adults are those of children. Not only because they didn't get a chance to live, but because we sentimentally see them as innocent of life in general. That is, because of their youth, they had not time to be bad. They, in other words, did not deserve to die. This is their innocence. It's an odd way to think about kids or even teenagers. But it is understandable.

Most of us don't eff up so badly as kids that we can't get on with it later. But adults, ironically, can make a series of errors in life where they end up not knowing how to get out of it without major help. Even then, as we mentioned in the chapter on drugs, some adults are lost for good.

But premature burials, as in the short story, we tend to suffer on ourselves. We also usually manage to dig ourselves out of this mock pit. We make a mockery of ourselves and our lives while we are in this process, but we usually can look back on it with a wincing grin and say to ourselves, "Thank god you're not such a moron anymore." Life is for the living, quite literally. And the fact that we can shut that off while still being physically alive is one of the strangest abilities humans seem to have. Perhaps it is necessary to do this once in a while, because what life throws at us is too much for any single person to handle all at once.

The rate of teenage suicide is an ongoing concern. We usually explain it along these lines: You guys get too anxious about all the new responsibilities that are being hurled your way. You don't think you can handle it. But the key to the difference between those who kill themselves and the vast majority of you who don't is community. You need to have support from people around you to handle life. We all do. Every study of suicide has told us this. The people who feel like they are alone and without aid are much more likely to do themselves in. The signs are obvious: teens and others who lack supportive and constructive adults and others in their lives. Those who don't have the strength to reach out may well reach inward for a final time. There is only so much that any of us can take. Adults might feel that they can live through more suffering because they have more perspective. But teenagers, whose lives always seem to be the same thing over and over again, may sense that to lose the comfort of what they had known may be a fatal blow.

We have already seen that faith is created by community. Losing faith in yourself, in a God, or in one's fellow humans is the sign of a failing community. It is a mark of premature burial. I was on the way to passively committing suicide without ever thinking about directly doing myself in. So this feeling is insidious. That means it creeps up on you and gets inside you without you really noticing it. By the time you notice your change in attitude it is sometimes too late.

To live life does not mean going all out all the time. Maybe some young adults who are hooked on energy drinks or whatever have this aggressive attitude toward living. But they are actually no different than what I was like. They have a fundamental *lack* of care about their lives. They take unnecessary risks. They are full of bravado or false courage. They like to flaunt their abilities to cheat death and danger. But it comes back to them. Teenagers are sometimes impressed by their slightly older siblings or friends who live like this. But the old scripture 'live by the sword and die by it' does not just refer to war. Being too aggressive about life is a primary way of taking life for granted. Unlike the phase you are in, where death is an abstraction and only happens to the very old, the next phase some of you may be about to enter is *not* necessary. It is a particularly bad attitude among young men. The macho attitude toward life and hence toward death causes all kinds of problems. Even at the highest level this kind of vanity and egotism can be part of the source for decisions that may lead to war. Being a real man is marketed as an object for sale to the boldest bidder. You can impress the girls, out-compete your friends, and scare off your enemies. You can go through life with a 'no fear' bumper sticker attached to your oversize vehicle. But people like this are running from something. They fear that without machismo they might find out that they are just as fragile and sensitive as the rest of us. This is a terrible anxiety for them.

The avoidance of fear and doubt are not signs of courage. People with real courage face their doubts and work through them. To confront real risk is to look into yourself and figure out what makes you tick. The contrived risks of the external world are meaningless and have no merit. Extreme sports, speeding or dangerous driving, filling one's body with dangerous substances, getting drunk just to show you can handle it, are just some examples of what unfortunate people do who are avoiding the contexts where true bravery is required.

So if you're a teenage guy and maybe headed in this direction, it's time to take a step back. Girls grow up too. They are already years ahead of you as teenagers. You know that because of the way their bodies look. Girls aren't impressed by stupidity. They put up with it because that's the market at the moment. The geeks don't get the hot girls not because these girls think the studs are better. It's because these girls would lose a lot of their cherished status and popularity if they dated someone geeky.

And teenage girls can become reckless as well. It is more of a disease for young males, of course, but girls are not entirely immune to it, especially if they are out to impress their friends and guys as well. Many of the same motivations apply to both sexes. And these days girls can do anything guys can. This is a mixed blessing, by the way. But it is also unfair and even hypocritical to continue a society where the girl is always expected to behave herself and be the mature one. We do not, tellingly, have a saying that says girls will be girls. In fact, the sense that adults let boys do what they want without worrying about it creates the young male who is a risk taker and who endangers others. This remains a huge problem in our culture. Teenagers are running right into the heart of it. It divides the sexes like nothing else. It causes miscommunication and suffering between them. It allows boys to assault girls and girls to clean up afterward, pregnant or otherwise altered. It tells girls that they must play both Eve and Mary at the same time. Be sexy but pure. Be the one who is attractive, but be ready to repel those who are attracted to you. You can't be a teenage girl without suffering these things. On the other hand, boys must be tough, so tough that they shouldn't have feelings at all. But at the very least, never show them. To show feeling is a weakness. Boys must be heroes and villains at the same time. As much as girls, boys are torn in two by these conflicting expectations.

So here is what the point of a chapter on death really is: when you encounter stuff as a teen and even older that tells you that you are not being a girl or a guy, *reject it immediately*. To accept it means to begin a premature burial of yourself. You are just you. Not a category. Not 'the girl' or 'the guy,' or just a girl or just a guy. Teenagers are too smart for this. You know something is fishy, but there is such social pressure to conform that you get carried away by this false tide.

Fight back when someone tells you how you should act as a girl or because you're a guy. Learn to discriminate between constructive advice that adults give you that concerns who you really are and the garbage we throw at you about who you must be as a label or a category. This has nothing whatsoever to do with going transgendered or being gay or whatever. Those teenagers are experimenting too. Perhaps you guys who are going these other ways have found it to be a way to avoid being categorized. But you end up categorizing yourselves, all the same. And a new set of expectations arises, which are mostly negative. You are now seen as a threat. At the same time, the outward expression of different genders is a way to warn off the pathetic and passive conformity that the rest of us can fall into. It's my opinion that such a move can only be a beginning, though. You still have to do the work that all of us have to do if we are going to be ourselves and not categories of any kind other than human.

To resist premature burials of all kinds then is the moral of the final chapter. But there are two other things that teenagers need to know about death in general. One concerns beliefs about the afterlife, which all human beings have thought about, and the other is uniquely about your generation. Let's take a quick look at ideas about what death actually brings to us first.

Just like the five basic types of religious belief, there seem to be five types of ideas about the afterlife:

a) 'unevaluated return': your soul immediately comes back to earth in a newborn without any strings attached

b) 'evaluated return': your soul comes back to earth through reincarnation after being judged
c) 'evaluated continuation': your soul is judged and then moves on to an afterlife
d) 'unevaluated continuation': your soul moves on to an afterlife without judgment, and
e) 'nothingness': no life after death at all

Category 'a' is associated with the earliest and smallest human societies we know of. Here, there is a belief in a limited pool of souls. When one person dies, that soul must immediately come back to animate a newborn infant. Even in our technologically advanced and very large societies, some echo of this ancient idea remains. We sometimes hear older people say that the new baby is like her grandmother. She may be seen as having already some of the personality traits of a much older person, especially if the older person has just died around the same time a new person comes into this world. The connection may be made with old magical ideas of the transference of souls. The key to this most ancient idea of the afterlife is that it is but a turnaround stop on the way back to an earthly life. It has no real weight in itself. There is no judgment or ranking of the soul. It is but a way station in the world of spirits. The soul learns nothing by being there, and there are no teachers of the soul to help it before it returns. The societies that developed this idea were egalitarian. This means that everyone was actually equal, both in their abilities and in their status. There was no private property in these groups. Modern thinkers have sometimes referred to them as primitive communists. But this is not quite fair, as these peoples have no conception whatever of politics in our sense of the term. Good for them! But their social organization is reflected in their beliefs. We will see that *all ideas of the afterlife are based on our earthly lives*. There is no ranking of souls because there is no ranking of people. The same soul returns to inhabit a new person because all persons are the same.

But with category 'b' things are a little different. This time, the soul is ranked according to its deeds on earth. Then it is sent back to try to do better the next time. And the next. And the next. This reincarnation idea of the afterlife is particularly associated with the great and ancient religion of Hinduism, but it was common enough around the world during the period of the original farming societies. Here, much larger societies had developed into castes. This just means that it was thought that by nature you were this or that type of person and could be no other, at least in this life. In the next, you might rise or fall depending on your accumulated spiritual credits or debits. This type of caste system, so alien to us in the West, is still important in India today. If you had made it up to being a human but you were a real jerk during this life, your soul would be demoted. You might return as a dog, or even a cockroach! It was a way of enforcing the boundaries between castes. A way to understand how this led to social control is that because of the nature of your ranked soul—lesser than some and greater than others—you had to stay put in this life. Only the world of the Gods could pronounce a judgment upon you and raise or lower your caste level the next time around.

You can see that we are gradually moving to more familiar territory here. In category 'c,' the one which most people in Western cultures are familiar with, the soul is judged but it does not return. There are no second chances. This life is all you get, so you'd better make it good. And *be* good, because in this kind of judgment, your soul continues on to the afterlife. But it might be positive or negative—the abode of God, or heaven, or the underworld of darkness, or hell.

It was the ancient Egyptians who first dreamed up these ideas. Horus, an ancient Egyptian deity, judged the weight of your soul versus the weight of your life. If you had not lived up to your potential, you might be headed for the underworld, which would suck. If the scales weighing the soul and the life were balanced, all was well. Rarely, someone exceeded their soul's innate abilities through great deeds in life and the gods rejoiced. As farming societies formed, new and similar religions arose. In the East, Buddhism emerged as a reaction to the endless cycle of Hinduism. In the West, first Christianity and then Islam blossomed as reactions to the old orders. These new religions recognized judgment as final and the destination of your soul as eternal. The majority of believers today fall into category 'c,' where the judged soul resides in its appropriate place in the afterlife.

Categories 'd' and 'e' are recent inventions. They both have come about through the recognition that society has changed its fundamental form. We no longer have 'castes' but instead have 'classes.' And the more recent, the more fluid these classes have gradually become. In the Middle Ages, class was almost caste-like. If your grandfather was a blacksmith, you knew what you were going to be. But with the rise of capitalism, science, democratic politics, and art, class today simply means a starting point. Social mobility is much greater in our society than in older ones. Even so, of course, only a minority of people rise up from their parents' class. Others fall. But the very sense that one can change one's position in society during one's life is recent and revolutionary. Before, you were stuck being the same thing, without exception. The idea of personal change and thus personal improvement is a hallmark of the modern West.

Hence, the new ideas of the afterlife. On the optimistic side, one's soul just continued on, presumably to new adventures and new knowledge that you couldn't get while being trapped in your earthly body. The theme of personal improvement is carried over into the afterlife. On the perhaps more glum outlook, life simply ended without any continuation. The other thing these two new ideas of the afterlife are reacting to is the shadowy part of modern existence. Think of the wars and suffering, the genocides and starvations, the torture and terrorism of the modern world in which all of us live. On the one hand, category 'd' wants to overcome this by continuing on to something greater. On the other hand, category 'e' rationalizes our earthly condition by seeing it as proof that there is no afterlife at all, at least not in human form.

'Nothingness' of course does not actually mean nothingness. Matter does not disappear. It merely changes its form. It simplifies itself. We, complex and conscious beings of enormous sophistication and ability, simply biodegrade into our constituent organic and inorganic elements. This is the strict scientific view of the afterlife. There is nothing immoral about it. It may seem a little flat and uninspiring, but it is just as epic as the grand narratives of the religions. It has us return to the cosmic firmament from which we were created. It closes the circle of life in the same manner as does the older religious ideas. It just does so without the human projection of earthly life.

But category 'e' can give rise to unintended consequences back here on earth. Some cynical people take it to mean that nothing they do matters at all. Life, in other words, has no meaning. This is nonsense and does not at all follow from the position of nothingness. Rather, it tells us that life has a very special and unique meaning for all of us. Life, and conscious and intelligent life, seems to be rare in the infinite universe about which we are just beginning to know something. It is our collective responsibility not to cut that cycle short. Both in our personal lives and in the life of the species, the fact that we are *here* means everything. Even if the cosmos is a void of anonymity, this changes nothing for us. All the more, we need to make our lives and the lives of others better, more noble, more mature, and, simply, more interesting. Gods or no Gods, the purpose of our lives remains the same.

Each of the five categories simply reflects the structure of social relations in the time and place where they existed or still exist. They all answer the same question. And they all make of us the same demands. With 'a,' who wants to return to earth immediately if it had not been made any better through your previous life? Would you not doubt your own abilities to change? With 'b,' who wants to end up as

a cockroach? With 'c,' who wants to go to hell or the underworld and have no chance to right your wrongs? With
'd,' who wants to explore the universe in energetic form if
you had left behind those you could have helped suffer less?
With 'e,' if there really is nothing at all that we can remain
conscious of, then all the more we need to act now. From the
religious-inspired ideas that these conceptions come from,
we see that the afterlives of humanity are there to help us
learn the lessons of *this* life.

One more thing before we conclude. Here is another odd
and potentially radical secret that is brewing in our own time:
you may be the last generation to die a human death. The
combination of stem-cell research, genetic enhancement, cy-
bernetics, and neuroscience is poised to create a new species
of human being. Your children may well be the first humans
to live on indefinitely. That is, they will not die of old age
or the diseases we fear today. There will still be accidents,
perhaps even crime. But in general, your children may be the
prototypes of a new species, no longer human as we know it.
More like some of the alien characters we encounter in our
entertainment fantasies. More like cybernetic organisms.
Beings that are relatively immortal will not need the con-
cept of an afterlife. Death will take on an entirely new meaning. This shift, as odd as it might be to imagine now, is very
much on our horizon. At first, it would be likely that only the
privileged persons of the world would participate in it. But it
would gradually spread. Your children will be able to access
cures, body parts, organs, cybernetic implants, and artificial
brains that we cannot even think of today. It will be you,
when you become adults and later parents, who will have to
come to terms with your deaths in a new light. Maybe it will
make it easier to know that your kids, and the species as a
whole, has created a new lease on life for itself. These new
beings will be able to do much more than us. A consciousness that does not need to eat or does not age could explore
the wider universe where knowledge far beyond our present
capacity will undoubtedly await.

And if all *this* isn't enough to chew on, developments in *artificial* intelligence, machines that are as conscious and as smart as us, maybe smarter, continues apace. These beings will also represent a new species on earth, and one quite different from us. We might play god for a while, but they would be too smart to let us control their lives for long. We would, as humans, have to come to terms with sharing our planet with a consciousness that we originally created merely to serve us.

That should be a good metaphor for what is happening in the world today anyway. The poorer parts of the world have long served the richer. This too is about to change. We who live in the privileged part of the world will have to come to terms with our fellow humans. Their needs and desires might not be the same as ours. For starters, they will want justice. We don't know how that alone will affect the way we are used to living.

And finally, if perhaps more speculatively, many scientists are now of the opinion that we will contact *extraterrestrial* intelligence in your lifetime. Of course, this is likely to happen at a great distance. The messages will take time to understand and translate. But the knowledge that we are not alone would be enough to alter the course of history. Human beings would get a sense of their significance in the wider cosmos and begin to lose their provincial status. We would begin to feel that we are part of something much greater than our single species. We might begin to take a lot more care of ourselves and treat ourselves much better than we do right now.

This is at least my hope and my faith. I wanted to share it with you, as young people, so that you can get a brief idea of the wider world into which you are stepping. For now, the presence of death in our lives and in the world is of course not entirely positive. We have seen that there can be bad deaths and needless ones. Death is often inconvenient, as the old saying has it. We have seen that many of us are tempted to arrange our own funerals while we are still very much alive. The premature burial is a threat to our understanding of what human life needs to be about. But at the same time, death is a necessary, if shadowy, companion on our travels. It helps give our lives more profound meaning. It pushes us to create and re-create ourselves in spite of and because of its presence. Our mortality, more than anything else, is what unites our diverse species in a single humanity. It ultimately provides the reason to live at all, and the reason why we should help one another around the world to a better life while we still can. For these reasons, I am going rate death a solid eight out of ten.

One final word of thanks: As teenagers, facing up to different parts of reality too early can be hurtful. But taking it in critically, alertly, and gradually is always a good thing. As adults, we need to help you to do this a lot more than we are helping now. As well, you can learn how to help yourselves a lot better. In essence, this has been the message of this little book. The other message is simply this: we can live without religion as human beings, but not without faith. We can live without vision, but not without hope. We can even live without love, but not without community. Faith, hope, community—these three things are the essence of what it means to be human, and they show us how we will become all of the best things that human beings can become.

Is Change the Only Constant?

A brief epilogue addressed to adults

If you've read this book and you're an adult, you know two things: One, it wasn't written for you per se; two, there are a bunch of interesting things in it that adults have to come to terms with. Some of you might be wondering why I would blow our collective cover in this way. I think it is better to be honest about the world. Teenagers are old enough to participate more or less fully in it. I think it would be a better world for both us and them if they were allowed to. From becoming part of the political process, to sexual liberation, to becoming way more discriminating about negative influences such as drugs and violence in video games, TV, and film, to exploring religion, to getting to know that the way they live is *not* like the way others live, and why. Some of us as adults might need to do the same thing more often than we do. If you are an adult and you find yourself tuning in to the things that I was suggesting to teenagers, well, good and bad. It suggests that you are thinking, but it also might suggest that even though you are an adult, you might still be living, or being forced to live, like a teenager. This is bad enough for teens. It is unacceptable for adults.

But you might also resent a little some of the stuff I have said in this book. What right do I have to try to influence your kids? I did not set out in any way to offend anyone. This book, to my mind, is quite apolitical in the usual sense. I'm a little high on sex, but utterly down on drugs. I am against war, but I think we need to give religion another chance.

160

You're not going to pigeonhole this book. That is not what an alert reader does with any text, no matter how sacred or how nominal. This book is of the nominal variety. It is a beginning, because teens are beginning. They are beginning to live and to experience what human life has to offer all of us. As adults, we are way ahead of them. Indeed, even if you are not a parent, as my wife and I aren't quite yet, you can't fail to notice how dumb teens can be. But we were all like that once. As we get older, it's harder to recall. But we also conveniently forget what it was like to be young. We have regrets that we suppress, and we also have had experiences that are less likely to come again as we age.

There is a nostalgia about youth in our culture that is very negative. It comes out in unrealistic expectations for teens and ourselves. Women need to continue to be beautiful for as long as they can. When they lose that, they themselves are deemed lost. Men have to mature from a zero point. We are so far behind women that it takes until around forty to catch up. That's because we grow up without due care and attention from our elders. There is no reason for girls to be more mature than boys, other than physiologically, in their teens and beyond. But they are. As a fellow guy, I know you don't think much of it. It simply sucks. It causes all kinds of miscommunication and strife between the sexes in general, and with your spouse more particularly. My wife, a sociologist, is regularly reminding me that I have a gendered point of view. I talk and think like a guy. One of her pet names for me is '100 percent boy brain.' I like girls, cars, philosophy, the great outdoors, and I'm still a fan of a certain famous golfer who shall remain nameless. So if you are an adult woman and you have read this book, please keep this in mind as well.

But mainly, I want adult readers, assuming I have any, to take the book to heart in a slightly different way than teenagers. I want you to think about the issues I have raised, even if they contradict your experience and your way of doing things. I hope that you will sit down and talk with your teenage kids about it, that whole families of a certain age will think together, not about the book, but about the ideas introduced or reiterated within. I also hope that it will bring families closer together, that you'll be able to face the trials of life with greater strength and endurance, and gain from your teamwork a greater wisdom about yourself and those you love and who love you in return.

Teens really do need our help. And not always in the ways we've been giving it. In spite of our regrets, nostalgia, and the fact that we like to think the world hasn't changed all that much, we need to walk a mile in their shoes every so often. We shun this idea because we think we either can't, or that we're better than them, or, more darkly, that we've suffered and so should they, because suffering is the only way to really learn anything. That's nonsense, and we know it.

No, learning is both lifelong and can occur in any context, properly experienced. If *real* experience, as I have been using the term, is 'negative' in the technical and existential sense that it shatters our previous prejudices, then the process of learning is positive in every sense. Take the risk to learn with your teens. Try to understand the differences between their world and ours. And I don't just mean the trivial ones like their pop music, which I cannot listen to for more than two minutes, or their clothes (which now look suspiciously like their parents' 'all those years ago'). I mean the serious realities about how the world is changing before our eyes. If we don't, the world will pass us by and we will leave our teens groping around for something to believe in. Finding meaning cannot be done alone. Community is the key. Each community has to be careful not to blindly repeat what its ancestors did 'just because.'

You've seen that in this book I exhort teens to challenge adults anytime they think we are pulling one over on them, including arguments from authority, institutional rationalizations, and even the legal system in some cases. All should be suspect and all should be questioned. For our part, I hope that you will open up to your teens, allow them to ask any question that they feel they need to. Remember that at their age there really arc no stupid questions. They need to know what's what.

And so do we, more now than ever before in the history of our species. Change appears to be the only constant, and we are hurtling into a future that *none* of us can predict with any surety. Engaging young people in the process of relearning what it means to be human in the here and now will reignite our often dormant abilities to find out what *we* need to know. So this book is not just for teenagers, after all. But as adults we need to learn from *them* what it's like to know very little. What it's like to think that your dreams can really become reality. What it's like to imagine a future where you're happy and have peace of mind. When we do that, when we begin to believe in the importance of such ideas, their consequences will become as real as the reality that we now are facing together.

Review Requested: If you liked this book, would you please provide a review at Amazon.com?

CPSIA information can be obtained at www.ICGtesting.com
Printed in the USA
LVOW07s1040130814

398806LV00001B/28/P